WE NEED TO DO THIS

UNIVERSITY OF CALGARY
LCR Publishing Services

WE NEED TO DO THIS

A History of the Women's Shelter
Movement in Alberta and the
Alberta Council of Women's Shelters

ALEXANDRA
ZABJEK

LCR Publishing Services
An imprint of University of Calgary Press
2500 University Drive NW
Calgary, Alberta
Canada T2N 1N4
press.ucalgary.ca

LIBRARY AND ARCHIVES CANADA CATALOGUING IN PUBLICATION

Title: We need to do this : a history of the women's shelter movement in Alberta and the Alberta
   Council of Women's Shelters / Alexandra Zabjek.
Names: Zabjek, Alexandra, author.
Description: Includes bibliographical references.
Identifiers: Canadiana (print) 2023047702X | Canadiana (ebook) 20230477046 | ISBN
   9781773854915 (hardcover) | ISBN 9781773854922 (softcover) | ISBN 9781773854953 (EPUB) |
   ISBN 9781773854946 (PDF) | ISBN 9781773854939 (Open Access PDF)
Subjects: LCSH: Alberta Council of Women's Shelters—History. | LCSH: Women's shelters—
   Alberta—History.
Classification: LCC HV1448.C32 A43 2023 | DDC 362.83/83097123—dc23

The University of Calgary Press acknowledges the support of the Government of Alberta through
the Alberta Media Fund for our publications. We acknowledge the financial support of the
Government of Canada. We acknowledge the financial support of the Canada Council for the Arts
for our publishing program.

Printed and bound in Canada by Imprimerie Gauvin
♻ This book is printed on Enviro paper

Copyediting by Andrew Goodwin
Cover Art: Women's shelter, 1972. Material republished with the express permission of Postmedia
   Network Inc. and the Provincial Archives of Alberta. Pattern overlay by Colourbox 6892418.
Cover design, page design, and typesetting by Melina Cusano

Contents

Foreword

"History is written by the victors," the saying goes, and it rings true when it comes to Canada.

Most of our old textbooks and history books were written by those with the power, the time, the will, and the means to write things down, thus forever reflecting and preserving events according to their perspective.

Right up until the twenty-first century, that perspective reflected and glorified the White man's world view, one that believed 'civilization' and 'progress' marched hand-in-hand with the colonizers.

Women, Indigenous peoples, and people of colour remain, at best, minor players in these narratives.

It's the first reason why I believe Alexandra Zabjek's book, *We Need To Do This*, is important.

Because the shelter movement is essentially a women's story.

Many good men funded and supported and helped build these institutions, but it was the passion, drive, and sheer hard work of women that got them off the ground and ultimately woven into the fabric of our social safety net.

It's a piece of our recent past that needs to be put on the record—for history's sake, for our children's sake—and shared.

Zabjek has done a masterful job of recording the voices and perspectives of the women of Alberta who founded these safe spaces for women and children.

The second reason *We Need To Do This* is important is because it gives voice to Indigenous and immigrant women's experiences within Alberta's shelter system.

When the Canadian shelter movement started to take off in the early 1970s, a significant number of Indigenous women took refuge in them, particularly in the West.

Yet their experiences and their cultures were often deeply misunderstood, or even ignored.

Ruth Scalp Lock remembers her early days working in a Calgary shelter. "I was the only Native counsellor there," she tells Zabjek. "They didn't know how to work with our women, especially to fulfill their spiritual needs. There were no workshops, and Elders did not come to work with the women. In our life, if you don't have that spirituality, you're just like a shell. There's nothing in there."

Scalp Lock also held a radically different viewpoint when it came to treatment and healing. At the time, second-wave feminists urged politicians to treat the abuse of women as a criminal offence, and non-Indigenous experts in domestic violence were calling on the justice system to criminalize abusive behaviour. Don't treat it as a private family matter, they implored police or judges who, for decades, had opted to stay out of peoples' marriages and let them somehow work it out themselves—often with tragic results.

But to someone like Scalp Lock, far too many Indigenous men were already in prison.

"All my brothers were survivors of residential school. Where are they today? They're six feet under. They never had the opportunity to deal with the sexual abuse they experienced at the residential school," she told Zabjek. "These issues are so deep-rooted. And where do men go to talk about these issues?"

To Scalp Lock, violence in the home was the result of generations of trauma, a toxic mix of racism, colonialism, and poverty. She and other Indigenous leaders sought a different, more holistic approach.

Scalp Lock would go on to help found Alberta's first off-reserve shelter for Indigenous women in 1993, now known as the Awo Taan Healing Lodge, in Calgary. Along with the women of the Alberta Council of Women's Shelters (ACWS), Indigenous shelter workers in Alberta ultimately developed innovative, cutting-edge programs aimed at men as well as women embroiled in domestic violence.

That innovation brings us to the third reason this book is important: it debunks the tired stereotype of Alberta as a redneck bastion of oil workers and cowboys. Alberta has always attracted and nurtured interesting, creative social justice pioneers like Jan Reimer, Edmonton's first female mayor and long-time executive director of ACWS. (When Reimer suggested in 2006 that Edmonton host a conference for the continent's shelter workers, her board responded by asking, "Why just the Americas? Let's do a world conference." So of course, they did.)

Zabjek gently reminds us that her province is full of contradictions. Albertans still revere former Premier Peter Lougheed, she writes, "a conservative who created a human rights commission and happily pumped money into the arts." She points out that former premier Ralph Klein, a pugnacious right-winger who fought against federal same-sex marriage legislation, was also a quiet and solid supporter of women's shelters.

Edmonton's beautiful river valley proudly commemorates its Famous Five feminists of the 1920s with a string of five parks named after Emily Murphy, Nellie McClung, Henrietta Muir Edwards, Irene Parlby, and Louise McKinney.

And just guess where the Toronto-based powerhouse editor of *Chatelaine* magazine of the 1960s and 70s, feisty feminist Doris Anderson, came from? Why, Medicine Hat, Alberta.

Clearly, in a history book centred on efforts to protect and shelter families from domestic violence, there is no 'victor.'

But *We Need To Do This* records an important piece of local history and is a thoughtful collection of stories and perspectives that need to be shared.

Alberta's shelter network—providing sanctuary and healing for generations of families—is a living testament to the perseverance, drive, and compassion of its women.

—Margo Goodhand is the former editor of the
Edmonton Journal and author of *Runaway Wives and Rogue Feminists:*
The Origins of the Women's Shelter Movement in Canada.

A Note on Terminology

Over the years, the language used to describe violence against women has changed as society and the sheltering movement have changed: wife battering, wife assault, abuse, domestic violence, violence against women, and intimate partner violence are all terms that have been used at different times. In this book, "domestic violence" will be used to include all forms of violence and abuse (not just physical violence) that happen within familial or intimate partner relationships. In addition, it should be noted that survivors may also experience abuse from parents, step-parents, siblings, grandparents, their children, extended family members, and other people who may be part of the household. Whatever terminology is used, the problem remains.

Domestic violence is a form of gender-based violence because women, girls, and gender-diverse people are at greater risk of experiencing it in their lifetimes. Gender-based violence is an issue faced by people all over the world; its prevalence is largely due to systemic gender inequality that disempowers those who identify as women, girls, and other gender minorities, stifles their voices so that their stories are not heard, takes away their dignity, safety, and human rights, and even normalizes these forms of violence.

Brenda Brochu has dedicated most of her working life to the women's shelter movement in Alberta. She was a founding board member of Odyssey House in Grande Prairie, the executive director of the Peace River Regional Women's Shelter for 15 years, and president of ACWS from 2013 to 2017.

No place to go

BRENDA

Brenda Brochu packed the truck at night: a crib, a highchair, some camp coolers to store milk for the baby. The kids were at the next-door neighbour's house, and her husband was on the night shift. Working alone, Brochu tried to keep her anxiety in check; after months of planning, it was time to leave her husband.

It was 1975. Brochu was a twenty-seven-year-old mother of two, living in Grande Prairie, a resource town that sits close to the B.C. border but remains a five-hour drive from Alberta's capital city. The town abuts thick swathes of boreal forest, and Brochu's husband was working at the big new pulp mill in town. The couple had moved to Alberta from Saskatchewan when the mill job opened up a few years prior.

Brochu was twenty-one years old when she got married; her husband was twice her age. "A great storyteller," she remembers. "Kind of volatile but very entertaining to listen to. When I was growing up, my mother was really the dominant figure and didn't treat my father that well. She was often dismissive toward him, and a lot of men in my family were quite taciturn. I didn't want that dynamic in my own marriage. I wanted a man who could stand up for himself, which my husband was."

But soon after their second child was born, that volatile personality turned into something different from what she had known. One day, he beat her, pounding her leg until it was black and blue. Their toddler witnessed the assault and was distraught for days afterward. "The way he tried to make up afterwards was not to apologize and say he wouldn't do it again," Brochu says. "Instead, he said, 'I wish I hadn't had to do that.'"

Brochu knew it would happen again, and she knew she had to find a way out.

The next weeks and months were spent planning her escape and—although she didn't know it at the time—it crystallized her understanding of what women fleeing domestic violence need and how woeful the services to help them were. In the mid-1970s, "wife-battering" was not front-of-mind as a widespread social problem. In fact, it was rarely discussed in public at all.

Brochu stashed away a few dollars here and a few dollars there, slowly building a $300 kitty in a way that wouldn't make her husband suspicious. At the same time, she was thinking of the profound ways her life would change once she was on her own. The baby needed to be weaned so she could go back to work. But first she'd need to find an apartment—and a job.

That night, while her husband was at work, Brochu focused on one task at a time: gathering her things, retrieving her kids from the neighbour's, and driving to the Swan Motel in town. When she finally walked into her motel room, after months of planning and mental preparation, Brochu felt a brief, yet distinct, moment of liberation—it would be days yet before the everyday challenges of life as a single mom, with a hostile ex-partner, would present themselves.

"I ended up in a one-bedroom basement apartment, so the two children slept in the bedroom and I slept on the couch. A lot of it was a very positive feeling—that I had managed to do this, that I had been able to get away and my kids were okay."

Grande Prairie was a city of about twenty thousand people at the time—not too small, but certainly not so big that Brochu could avoid her ex-husband. She remembers that he eventually contacted her, wanting to see the children. He would pick the kids up for Saturday visits. On one such weekend, he refused to bring them back, abducting them to British Columbia and, through an intermediary, demanding that Brochu return to the marriage. She was terrified. At the time, custody orders were not enforced across provincial borders, and she felt she could do nothing but wait until he returned to Alberta with her children.

Brochu's husband returned to Alberta about a week later because the kids had come down with chicken pox, at which point Brochu saw her opening. She made an excuse that she needed to take their daughter to the doctor. She went to his apartment to get the children.

"I had the children in the car and I was backing out of the driveway when my husband opened the door, slammed his foot over mine on the brake and put his hands around my neck. I screamed and someone called the police."

The couple ended up in family court that day, and Brochu was given interim custody of the children. For the next several years, she lived in constant fear that her children might be abducted again, all the while trying to settle into the rhythms of a single mother.

At the time, Brochu was working as a reporter for the *Daily-Herald Tribune*. She had walked into the offices of the newspaper soon after leaving her husband, armed with a modest journalism resume from before her children were born. In the mid-1970s, Grande Prairie was bustling, and Brochu was hired immediately.

The oil boom that had been rumbling through many parts of the province was about to hit Grande Prairie hard. In 1976, a natural gas field was discovered about thirty kilometres west of the city. It changed the face and feel of the town. As a reporter, Brochu learned that a boom doesn't just bring jobs and money: it also brings an influx of workers, sometimes more than a mid-sized Alberta city can handle.

"All the hotel rooms and motel rooms were full of oil patch workers, and even the campground was full. It wasn't just tourists or people passing through—it was working people tenting in the campground because they couldn't find any other accommodations," Brochu remembers.

"I realized then that if another woman was in the same position that I had been in, she would not have been able to do what I did. She would not have been able to save up a few dollars to stay in a motel until she had a job and an apartment—because there was no place to go."

The realization struck Brochu with such clarity that she knew she had to do something for that unknown woman. She attended a community meeting in town and pitched the idea of opening a house that would serve as a refuge for women fleeing violence in their homes. Almost immediately she began hearing stories from others who had also witnessed or experienced abuse. It was the start of a years-long journey toward opening a women's emergency shelter in Grande Prairie, which makes Brochu a pioneer in a movement that would change the lives of women across Alberta forever.

—Brenda Brochu was instrumental in advocating for a women's shelter in Grande Prairie. Croken House (later renamed Odyssey House) opened in 1980. It was the third women's shelter in the province, after the Calgary Women's Emergency Shelter (CWES) and the first Women In Need (WIN) House in Edmonton. Brochu was a founding member of the board of directors for Croken

House and later went on to work with WIN House I in Edmonton and then the Peace River Regional Women's Shelter. She also spent four years as president of the Alberta Council of Women's Shelters.

֍ ֍ ֍

In 1975—the year Brenda Brochu gathered her children and snuck away from her home under a night sky—delegates gathered in Mexico City for the first United Nations World Conference on Women. The meeting occurred against a backdrop of international politics, which featured a notable lack of support for the event from UN member states and fears that the participants themselves would split between economically developed and less-developed nations.[1]

The conference received scant coverage in the Alberta press, where discussions of feminism were typically relegated to the "lifestyle" or "family" sections of the major daily newspapers. That's where the Ann Landers advice column held a regular spot, perched next to predictable features on interior design and homemaking. Feminism, in other words, was just another women's issue that men were not expected to care about or view as news. In mid-1970s Alberta, the front-page story was the oil and gas boom. There were grand promises of infrastructure mega-projects that would bring extraordinary investment, a plethora of jobs, and endless possibilities for resource extraction. With streams of black gold coming out of the ground, a rush of men and money was coming in.

But the wealth wasn't evenly distributed. During boom times, the male-dominated oil and gas sector compensates labour in an over-the-top way, and those excluded from the sector are left even further behind. Full-time female workers in the 1970s in Alberta earned about fifty-nine cents for every dollar that men earned.[2] Even in the public service, women weren't doing much better. Women earned roughly 65 per cent of their male counterparts' salaries, according to a study commissioned by the Alberta Human Rights Commission in 1979. The government at the time explained the difference as resulting from "technical deficiencies" in the research, and the

---

1   Suzanne de Lesseps, "Women Push for Rights." *Calgary Herald,* June 21, 1975, 7.

2   Linda Trimble, "The Politics of Gender in Modern Alberta," in *Government and Politics in Alberta,* ed. Allan Tupper and Roger Gibbins (Edmonton: University of Alberta Press, 1992), 221.

commission itself rejected recommendations to promote greater equality in government workplaces.[3]

Such glaring economic inequalities had been a key focus of the Royal Commission on the Status of Women that swept across Canada after its appointment by Prime Minister Lester B. Pearson in 1967. The commission was tasked with considering how the federal government could ensure women equal opportunities in all aspects of Canadian society. For a start, it proposed the then-radical idea that women should be able to choose whether or not to work outside the home.[4] While Canadian women had the right to work—and many did—employers could openly discriminate on the basis of sex, and long-entrenched social norms meant that most women still married young and had children, and the man was the default breadwinner in the family. Indigenous women, women of colour, and those living in poverty had an even harder time securing full-time employment in the face of outright discrimination and of structural barriers, such as lack of access to transportation or reliable childcare, that hinder workforce participation.

The myriad obstacles and Catch-22's that tumble from the premise of offering women the option to work were explored over the course of the report's almost 500 pages: the need for a national daycare strategy; the need for paid maternity leave; the need for effective equal pay laws. The commission formed an integral part of the swell of second-wave feminism building across the country, and indeed the world. Women were critically evaluating their place in a thoroughly patriarchal society and exposing the many layers of systemic discrimination that kept them there. At the same time, Black women, Indigenous women, lesbians, and others faced even more layers of discrimination, from society as a whole and sometimes from the women's movement itself, which was often dominated by White, heterosexual women.

By the early 1970s, women were organizing. In the spring of 1970, an abortion "caravan" travelled from Vancouver to Ottawa, the first national demonstration of the second-wave feminist movement in Canada. The lead vehicle carried a coffin filled with coat hangers, representing the women who had died from dangerous, illegal abortions. Though birth control and abortion had been legalized in Canada the year before, restrictions on access,

---

3   Linda Goyette, "Gov't Pays Women Less, Report Says," *Edmonton Journal*, October 15, 1979, 17.

4   *Report of the Royal Commission on the Status of Women in Canada*, https://publications. gc.ca/site/eng/9.699583/publication.html, xii.

especially access to abortion, were prohibitive. The caravan stopped in cities along the way to Ottawa, prompting rallies and meetings with feminist organizers in places like Calgary and Edmonton. The caravan arrived on Parliament Hill on Mother's Day weekend; hundreds of women marched on Parliament Hill before part of the group branched off to protest at Prime Minister Pierre Elliott Trudeau's residence at 24 Sussex Drive, leaving the coffin behind when they left. When the House of Commons reconvened that Monday, the lawmakers found a group of women protesting inside the House, shouting, "Free abortion on demand!"

The caravan was organized by the Vancouver Women's Caucus, one of the earliest women's liberation groups in the country; it wanted to mobilize women around issues of equal pay, childcare, abortion, and birth control.[5] Another powerful feminist group to emerge in Vancouver in the early 1970s was Vancouver Rape Relief, which started out by running a twenty-four-hour crisis line for women who had experienced sexual or physical assault. A similar service was being run in Ontario by the Toronto Rape Crisis Centre. These groups wanted to make body politics part of the mainstream conversation, highlighting the ways Canadian women were not in control of their own bodies, either through legislation that limited their reproductive choices or social attitudes that deferred to the adage that "boys will be boys" in the face of assault and harassment.

Like its provincial politics more generally, feminist organizing in Alberta was unique. Some of the most prominent Alberta feminists of the era were Indigenous women, like Nellie Carlson, Kathleen Steinhauer, and Jenny Margetts, who founded the group Indian Rights for Indian Women, to fight against sections of the Indian Act that stripped Indigenous women of their Indian status and Treaty rights if they married non-status men. In Edmonton, Susan McMaster and Sharon Batt began publishing the feminist periodical *Branching Out*, which offered space for women's writing—and their activism—to appear on newsstands across the country, attracting writers such as Margaret Atwood. In 1975, activists in both Edmonton and Calgary were spearheading plans to open rape crisis centres, despite governments that refused their requests for funding. Other organizations like the Calgary Status of Women Action Committee were focused on issues like workplace equity

---

5   Judy Rebick, *Ten Thousand Roses: The Making of a Feminist Revolution* (Toronto: Penguin, 2005), 35.

and matrimonial property rights. The committee lobbied for the establishment of a provincial advisory council on the status of women but faced such intense government opposition that the group eventually shifted its mandate to become a coordinator for local women's organizations. In Edmonton, the group Options for Women focused on maternity leave rights, which yielded new—but largely insufficient—legislation to ensure women could take leave from their jobs after giving birth. These regional organizations were succeeded by the Alberta Status of Women Action Committee, which formed in 1976 as the first provincial feminist organization in Alberta.[6]

But even in the mid-1970s, as feminist organizations gained traction and attention, many Alberta women were still reluctant to associate themselves with the most public demonstrations of mainstream feminism. It wasn't uncommon to hear disdain for "women's libbers" by those who would breezily dismiss all feminists as radicals with unrealistic ideals. That characterization was sometimes internalized. "The women of Alberta are emphatically not part of the Women's Movement—or so they say," reporter Heather Menzies wrote in the *Edmonton Journal* in 1975.[7] "They see it as a bunch of women burning their bras and 'going out and storming places', as one representative woman put it. They consider it 'too pushy . . . too radical . . . and too sensational'."

If the general public in Alberta wasn't willing to embrace the feminism championed by authors-turned-celebrities such as Gloria Steinem, it most certainly wasn't paying much attention either to the struggles of Indigenous women, Black women, lesbians, or women with disabilities. At the time, Indian Rights for Indian Women was working alongside groups like the Voice of Alberta Native Women's Society, which was fighting against the continued placement of Indigenous children in White foster homes and against sexism within their own band councils. In the years before politician Rosemary Brown ran for the federal NDP leadership, her speeches were often relegated to the "Family Living" section of the *Calgary Herald*. As the first Black woman ever elected to a legislative chamber in Canada, Brown gave speeches on the specific struggles that resulted from being Black and being a woman,[8] and she critiqued female politicians who did little to improve the lives of all

---

6   Lois Harder, *State of Struggle* (Edmonton: University of Alberta Press, 2003), 23-29.

7   Heather Menzies, "Liberation in Low Gear," *Edmonton Journal*, December 30, 1975, 9.

8   "Women's Lib Helps Black Men Too–MLA Rosemary Brown," *Calgary Herald*, April 12, 1973.

women—not just wealthy and White women.[9] This work was covered in the back pages of the *Herald*, the articles placed next to advertisements for rummage sales and women's fashion.

Even the Royal Commission on the Status of Women, which heard from hundreds of women across the country with the authority of a national inquiry, was criticized in Nova Scotia for not doing enough outreach to Black and Indigenous Maritimers, who faced issues of poverty and isolation.[10] The second wave of feminism wasn't a tidy narrative of women unanimously organizing and uniting. There were socialist feminists and radical feminists, the former believing that true social change for women would be tied to an overhaul of the capitalist system, while the latter believed that women's liberation would be achieved by challenging and ultimately dismantling patriarchal norms in every institution and within every gendered relationship. As feminists met and organized, other cleavages were revealed, across lines of race, class, and sexual orientation. Indigenous women, Black women, lesbians, and others were forming their own organizations, centering their own stories and their own ideas for achieving equality and justice for their communities. "I am not interested in gaining entry to the doors of the 'White women's movement,'" wrote the famed Stó:lō writer and academic, the late Lee Maracle. "I would look just a little ridiculous sitting in their living rooms saying 'we this and we that.' . . . I say this for those Native women who think they may find equal relations among White women and who think that there may be some solace to be found in those relations."[11]

Women were wrestling with the weighty issues of how to improve their social, economic, and physical environments, all central to the feminist cause, despite a lack of support from peers and institutions. As Menzies noted in the *Edmonton Journal*, Alberta women might not have always wanted to publicly declare themselves feminists, but they still cared deeply about the issues at play. Even in that climate, there was one poster cause that women in the province were widely willing to stand up for, perhaps because it began in a place familiar to many in a province covered in swathes of wheat and canola: the family farm. It was the case of Irene Murdoch, who familiarly became known as the "Nanton Farm Wife."

---

9   "Women Could Set Own Political Rules," *Calgary Herald*, June 18, 1973, 13.

10   Rosemary Speirs, "Lacklustre Hearings Dull and Repetitive," *Calgary Herald*, September 19, 1968, 27.

11   Lee Maracle, *I Am Woman* (Richmond, BC: Press Gang Publishers, 1996), 18.

✳ ✳ ✳

Irene Murdoch married her husband, Alex, in 1943. The couple worked on ranches in southern Alberta for a few years until they were able to purchase their own. Over the years, they bought bigger and bigger tracts of land and, according to both, their hard work allowed their operations to flourish and fortunes to grow.

At some point the relationship began to crumble; by 1968, Irene Murdoch had filed for separation and a claim for a portion of the couple's assets. But the courts repeatedly denied that Irene Murdoch had any legitimate stake in the ranching business she had spent twenty-five years building through physical labour and business deals. For five months every year, as Irene Murdoch told the court, her husband left their home to work for a stock association and she headed the ranch herself. Even when her husband was home, her work included "[h]aying, raking, swathing, moving, driving trucks and tractors and teams, quietening horses, taking cattle back and forth to the reserve, de-horning, vaccinating, [and] branding."[12]

A trial judge dismissed her efforts as "the work done by any ranch wife," offering an implicit acknowledgment that the work was simultaneously ex-pected and valueless. After fighting for three years through three levels of court, Irene Murdoch was left with nothing more than "a pile of legal bills and $200 a month, for a lifetime of hard labour."[13] The Supreme Court even found that Irene Murdoch should pay a portion of her husband's legal costs. It wasn't until more than a year later, after launching another court proceeding, this time for divorce, that Irene Murdoch was awarded a financial settlement worth approximately one third of her ex-husband's total financial assets.

The Nanton Farm Wife was widely discussed in Alberta and beyond; academics such as Lois Harder wrote that her story represented "the central focus for feminist organizing" in Alberta in the 1970s.[14] While the case was front and centre in the fight for matrimonial property law reform, an import-ant detail of Irene Murdoch's experience was omitted in most accounts of her story. One night, as husband and wife argued over their ranch and who

12   Supreme Court of Canada, Murdoch v. Murdoch (1975) 1 S.C.R. 423, 1973-10-02, 443.
13   Margo Goodhand, *Runaway Wives and Rogue Feminists: The Origins of the Women's Shelter Movement in Canada* (Halifax and Winnipeg: Fernwood Publishing Company, 2017), 70.
14   Harder, *State of Struggle*, 2.

owned what, Alex Murdoch's anger turned violent: he broke his wife's collar-bone and her jaw in three places and sent her to the hospital. The dissenting judge in the Supreme Court Case, Bora Laskin, described the incident as a "physical clash."

"It was a great case for the feminist movement at the time because it was so grossly unfair and so clearly sexist, that a spouse's contributions could be completely ignored in the end," says Margo Goodhand, author of *Runaway Wives and Rogue Feminists: The Origins of the Women's Shelter Movement in Canada.* "But when I read Laskin's comments about the injuries she suffered that last night in the home, it triggered a whole new way of looking at the case. No one at the time wrote about Irene's last hours in her home—but they must have been horrific.

"Those other facts were irrelevant, and maybe shameful to Irene herself because she never talked about the assault either, or let her lawyers use it in subsequent court appeals."

In the early 1970s, domestic violence simply wasn't widely discussed in Canada. The home was considered a private sphere, where men paid the bills and ultimately controlled what happened there. If a man hit or beat his wife, the immediate question that many people asked was, "What did she do to provoke him?" These patriarchal attitudes reverberated through the social fabric of Canada. Women's bodies, through restrictions on birth control and abortion, were still regulated by mostly male legislators; it would take another decade before marital rape would even become a crime in Canada. In such an environment, is it any surprise how few people were willing to acknowledge that physical abuse was happening in suburban bungalows, Prairie farm-houses, and inner-city apartments?

At that time, when women came forward about abuse, or others learned of it, the response was typically muted. Social workers promoted reconcilia-tion between spouses, no matter the marital circumstances. Doctors treated broken bones but didn't ask why a woman was making multiple visits to the emergency ward. Police would sometimes take a man out of the home to "cool off," but wouldn't follow through with formal charges.

For those experiencing violence in the home, there was—as Brenda Brochu and so many others have observed—no place to go.

"My mother had no education, she had nine babies, she had no employ-ment skills or experience. So she stayed and she took it. There were holes in the walls, there were bruises, black eyes, all that stuff," says Heather King, who grew up in Grande Prairie and was one of the first staff members at Croken House. "We would have incidents where we were running to the neighbours, calling the police, hiding in the basement, clinging to each other and crying. We had everything packed under the bed for probably twelve years, ready to leave my father, but my mother had no options."

In a twist of sad and strange irony, King's mother often opened her home to other women experiencing violence—women she met through her husband's attendance at Alcoholics Anonymous. It was an example of how women with few resources, struggling in their own lives, are often the first to step up to help peers in need. King's sister once remarked that their mother had the first de facto women's shelter in Grande Prairie, long before Brenda Brochu and members of the Grande Prairie Women's Residence Association opened a formal shelter on Main Street.

For thousands of women in Alberta's smallest hamlets and biggest cities alike, the "options" were similar: stay at a friend's house, sleep in your car, run to a neighbour when things are especially terrifying. Towns might have had animal shelters, but there were no shelters for women in need of refuge. Sometimes, friends and neighbours of abused women didn't want to get involved for fear an angry husband would show up on their doorstep. But often, women like Heather King's mother helped others in need, readying a bed for a neighbour or quietly driving a friend to the doctor.

Even years later, after the first women's shelters had opened in urban centres, women in more rural areas relied on their ingenuity to help their sisters, friends, and neighbours. Before there was a physical shelter in Rocky Mountain House, staff of the Mountain Rose Shelter used their own vehicles to drive women to the closest facility with an available bed—often almost a hundred kilometres away in Red Deer.

"There wasn't anything happening in government. No one was saying, 'We identify this issue. Let's start some projects in these communities,'" says Pat Lowell, who sat on a steering committee to determine the feasibility of a shelter in Pincher Creek in southern Alberta and later became a shelter board member. "It was totally the opposite of that. It was the grassroots saying, 'We need to do this.'"

Through her job as a reporter for the *Herald-Tribune* in Grande Prairie, Brenda Brochu heard about a meeting being organized by the United Church, which wanted to sponsor a project to benefit the community. Brochu was intrigued and went to the meeting, not as a reporter, but as a citizen who had a vague but pressing idea for an endeavour that she knew would help many in her town, especially as rents were jacked up and hotel rooms filled in the midst of the energy boom. Inspired, she stood up and told the crowd that women needed a safe place to stay if they were fleeing abuse in their homes.

She soon met others who had either experienced domestic violence themselves or had seen their mothers being abused. They made connections with local politicians such as MLA Elmer Borstad and secured a major donation from a town councillor—a pink house that sat kitty-corner to the Co-op on the main drag in town. Croken House, named after former town councillor John Croken, opened in 1980. The shelter started as a space to help homeless, transient, and abused women, but it soon became clear that domestic violence was so widespread and harmful that the shelter would focus its efforts to help those affected by it.

"My involvement in the sheltering movement is one of the most worthwhile things I've ever done in my life. Getting a shelter started in Grande Prairie is one of the things I'm most proud of," says Brochu.

⚘ ⚘ ⚘

This book tells the stories of women who paved similar paths to that of Brenda Brochu, even if their surroundings were very different. They come from Banff and Bonnyville, High Level and High River, and everywhere in between. They are White women, Indigenous women, and women who weren't born in Canada. Some started their work in the 1970s, while others later built upon the efforts of their peers.

Their work emerged in lockstep with the broader feminist movement as it evolved in Canada, but it also played out within the unique social and political context of Alberta. When the Calgary Women's Emergency Shelter opened in 1973, it was among the first women's shelters in the country that focused on helping women escaping domestic violence. In the 1980s, women in smaller Alberta centres networked with decision-makers in their communities to gain support for women's shelters at a time when "feminism" and "special interests" were looked down upon by male-dominated municipal and provincial governments. In the 1990s, Indigenous women in Alberta advocated for shelters to serve their sisters, whose experiences are shaped by the intergenerational effects of colonialism and systemic racism. At the same time, all shelters were working within a political climate that normalized the slashing of social service budgets. Despite these challenges, shelters, over time, developed more nuanced understandings of domestic violence that allowed them to establish cutting-edge programs to help women and children in crisis.

The women and men who have been part of this movement changed the public's perception of domestic violence and the government's view of its responsibility to help them. The earliest shelters recognized that there was strength in numbers, and in 1983 they officially incorporated the Alberta Council of Women's Shelters. The organization has for decades acted as a central voice of advocacy, not only for adequate shelter funding, but also for legal reforms and data-driven policies to ensure women fleeing domestic violence are safe and supported.

Shelters have changed dramatically over the past four decades: the buildings are better designed and equipped, the staff are better trained, and the policies are better developed. There are still struggles for adequate funding and appropriate facilities, and misogynist attitudes persist in Canada, endangering the safety of women in various ways. But the shelter movement continues to build on the early efforts of those who didn't always know what would happen when they joined a social movement that changed the lives of Alberta's women for the better.

In the early 1970s, Ardis Beaudry worked tirelessly along with other early volunteers to find safe spaces for women in distress in Edmonton—anywhere and wherever they could. These beds from a shelter in 1972 showcase the cramped and limited spaces available to women.

A reckoning about wife battering

ARDIS

Ardis Beaudry climbed the winding staircase to the bell tower of the All Saints' Anglican Cathedral in downtown Edmonton. The corridor was uncomfortably narrow and steep, but she pushed ahead. It was 1970, and it was Beaudry's first shift at the first shelter for women in the city.

Beaudry had no experience as a social worker or a shelter employee, but she was willing to volunteer and, in the early 1970s, that was qualification enough. The bell tower was small and isolated, hardly an ideal spot for an overnight shelter, but it had room for a few pieces of furniture and a coffee maker, so it would have to do. The church had been the first to offer space to an upstart organization trying to create a shelter for women in crisis, so the group took it. That night, a social worker brought in the first client—an intoxicated woman who promptly fell asleep—and Beaudry was relieved. She didn't know what she would have done had the woman tried to leave.

Outside that bell tower, Beaudry's life was that of stay-at-home mother, judge's wife, and volunteer with the Catholic Women's League. She got involved with the church organization after moving to the provincial capital as a new bride who didn't know a soul. A friend told her to contact the Catholic Women's League, and that's where she met a circle of friends, including Daisy Wilson, a natural 'doer' who would invite friends for tea to discuss new projects or pressing concerns.

A few years before that night in the bell tower, Wilson had told her friends about an observation that concerned her. "Daisy had a real worry about the young women who were coming into town on the bus," Beaudry remembers. "She felt they were being picked up before they got out of the Greyhound bus depot by men who were waiting around. It was the 1960s, and young girls were starting to travel across Canada. She could see that a lot of Indigenous girls were arriving, often looking for family. And if there was nobody there that could help them, they'd be picked up before they could even get out of the depot."

The group pinpointed a glaring gender disparity in the city: there was a shelter for men who had no place to go, but nothing equivalent for women. Beaudry and her friends felt compelled to help the women who Wilson had observed at the bus depot, but it would take months before they formalized the idea of starting a drop-in space for vulnerable women, and even more time before they realized that, for many of these women, their own homes were unsafe places to be.

Beaudry and Wilson started organizing, calling the YWCA and every other social service organization they could think of that served women, including the Edmonton Social Planning Council. It took months until they got some organizational backing to open a drop-in shelter, where women could rest and get a cup of coffee, maybe make a few phone calls. They initially secured a small amount of funding from church groups and launched their endeavour in the All Saints' Cathedral in January 1970. Over the next several months they saw dozens of women, including teenagers. Some came to the shelter inebriated; others were suffering from physical injuries or ailments; still others were just looking for a temporary place to rest while they tried to secure their next move.

"The bell tower was right downtown, so it was in a good location, but we knew right away it was not an ideal situation. We couldn't keep going up those stairs—it was dangerous. So, we got moved into the basement of the church. We were moving from pillar to post," says Beaudry.

The group later bounced between a few downtown locations, landing in a storefront that had once housed a pawnshop. They laid down mats for women to sleep on, while a skeleton staff and volunteers tried their best to refer women to more formal service agencies. There was no hot water and no showers, but it was the only option for women with nowhere else to go, so they were always busy. Beaudry remembers asking the government for money: "And we were very much told that women should stay home."

The group eventually managed to secure meager, haphazard funding through different organizations and from provincial and municipal governments. It was a constant learning process for those who managed and staffed the shelter: they learned by doing and, sometimes, by failing. "There were two really young staff with the Edmonton Social Planning Council who tried to help us find locations—and here we were, these housewives," says Beaudry. "More and more girls started dropping in. We had a volunteer staff, which was not too good because the volunteers sometimes didn't show up and sometimes they didn't know what they were doing any more than any of us knew what we were doing."

By 1974, the provincial government had finally recognized the dire situation of vulnerable women in Edmonton. That year, the minister of health and social development announced a contract with the City Centre Church Corporation, a local charity, to operate a new facility, called the Women's Emergency Accommodation Centre, for homeless and transient women. It was a blow for Beaudry's group, which had formalized their organization by incorporating as the Edmonton Women's Shelter Ltd. (EWS) the year prior. They felt they still had a role to play, however, and dreamed of opening a house that could offer women more freedom than they might find at a homeless shelter. They decided to narrow their focus to help women who had experienced domestic violence.

At the time, Beaudry was just learning that many women without housing were fleeing abuse in their families. "We had no idea how much abuse was around. At the beginning, I was in shock because I just couldn't believe what I was hearing," she says. "I think you realize that you have to stick together. I really learned to listen because who was I to say, 'I don't believe what you're telling me.' You just don't know."

At the same time, Beaudry was navigating her new role as activist and advocate while maintaining her life as a stay-at-home mother to four children and wife of a husband with a demanding job. "My husband never said anything about me not doing this work, so I guess I took it for granted that it was okay. I got my own car, so he must have been okay with it—either that or he got tired of me driving him to work and talking about it," she laughs. Years later, while looking through a stack of documents at home, Beaudry found an envelope with her husband's name on it. Inside, there were work papers that showed her husband had asked for a presentation about family violence in his capacity as a judge. Beaudry is still incredulous at the discovery: "He never said a word about that to me."

Edmonton Women's Shelter Ltd. was also learning to navigate the world of non-profit partnerships and fundraising. It connected with the Clifford E. Lee Foundation, which urged the women to find an appropriate house that could be used as a shelter for women. Meanwhile, the group continued to lobby the provincial government for funds and launched a public fundraising campaign that lasted for months. By fall of 1978, EWS was getting ready to open the doors of a brand-new facility for women in Edmonton.

On December 5, 1978—eight years after the first drop-in night at the All Saints' Cathedral and four years after Edmonton Women's Shelter Ltd. was pushed out of operating the first government-funded homeless women's shelter in Edmonton—the first WIN House opened. It was named Women In Need, and it would serve women fleeing domestic abuse.

"When you think back on it, this all began because one woman cared enough to help somebody else," says Beaudry. "That's often what happens. One person has an idea or does something that starts a whole movement."

—Ardis Beaudry was a long-time board member for WIN House, a founding member and the first president of the Alberta Council of Women's Shelters, and an honourary member of ACWS. Beaudry worked tirelessly for the shelter movement for decades after that first night volunteering in the bell tower of the All Saints' Anglican Cathedral. She passed away in 2021.

❦ ❦ ❦

In the 1970s, women across the country were organizing. They spanned the spectrum, from young women publicly tossing their high heels into trash cans, to Black women fighting for recognition that both race and gender affected their lives and livelihoods, to married women like Ardis Beaudry and the members of the Catholic Women's League who approached their work from a position of benevolence and a sense of social justice, wanting to address the gaps in services for women in need. But as different as their backgrounds and political perspectives may have been, many women's groups—once they gathered, listened, and talked—shared a common experience: a discovery that domestic violence was widespread and women needed help.

Whether it was through the medium of a rape crisis line, women's centre, or homeless shelter, it soon became apparent that women seeking help often needed to escape violence at home. "When women's centres opened in communities across Canada, these were supposed to be political action hubs for feminism," says Nancy Janovicek, a professor of history at the University of Calgary. "Then when women would come to them, they'd say, 'I need help getting out of this abusive relationship.' And they realized there was nowhere to refer them."

In Edmonton, the path to a women's shelter for those escaping domestic violence began in 1968, when twenty-eight social agencies and church groups gathered to discuss the housing needs of transient women. This was the group that Ardis Beaudry and Daisy Wilson had helped to convene; they were joined by established organizations like the YWCA and operated under the direction of Ronald Mossman, a well-known Quaker and social justice organizer in the city. Over the course of a year, the coalition researched what services were available for vulnerable women in Edmonton. Their final report, called the Mossman Report, outlined different categories of women, such as "Girls With Pathological Problems - e.g., Prostitutes, Alcoholics" and "Girls Released From Institutions Who Need Supervised Residential Accommodation." The use of the term "girls" to refer to women who often had husbands and children of their own was at once infantilizing and problematic, but also reflective of the attitudes of the era.

Under the category of "Destitute Girls Coming To The City" was this note: "Many of the destitute girls who come to the City express a great need to get away from their homes for many tragic reasons. Often it is because of beatings, etc., by a cruel husband. These frantic women feel trapped and are trapped. They require short-term housing, sometimes with babysitting available."[1] The report called for more supportive housing units for young women and for the establishment of a 24/7 'point of contact' for newcomers to the city to receive information about social services and housing options.

That domestic violence was reduced to a footnote in an expansive report on vulnerable women was not surprising in the 1960s and 1970s. The issue simply wasn't widely discussed. When it was, stereotypes and myths were almost always present: women had done something to provoke their husbands' anger; the real problem was alcohol; violence was an issue for poor people. These notions dominated the narrative at the time, as they sometimes still do today.

It wasn't until 1982 that a House of Commons committee would produce a report called "Wife Battering: Report on Violence in the Family." Even then,

---

1   *The Mossman Report on Housing Needs in the City of Edmonton for Homeless Girls 15-25 Years of Age,* May 1969, 2.

the first page of the document sets up the parameters of the problem by acknowledging that living with someone can be "frustrating".

"Nerves become frayed, tempers flare, dishes start flying about the room and someone gets slapped. Such events are not pleasant, but they are not unexpected; they are tolerated, and wryly made fun of. . . . We have found that wife battering is not a matter of slaps and flying crockery. Battered women are choked, kicked, bitten, punched, subjected to sexual assault, threatened, and assailed with weapons," the report states.[2]

Considering that elected members of Parliament thought slapping one's spouse was a normal, almost expected, event in the course of marriage, it's perhaps not surprising that even early advocates of women's shelters, like Ardis Beaudry, had lots to learn about the realities of domestic violence. Some of these advocates struggled to understand even the basics of the phenomenon, let alone sympathize with women who didn't "just leave."

Rose-Marie McCarthy joined EWS not out of a personal desire to advance the cause of fighting domestic violence, but because Beaudry, a good friend, had asked her. "I knew how to take notes," she says simply. McCarthy remembers carefully cranking out meeting minutes on a Gestetner duplicating machine, her recollection of that time-consuming process just as firmly etched in her memory as the discussions she was recording. She bristles at the notion that she was either "rogue" or a "feminist", as the title of journalist Margo Goodhand's book, *Runaway Wives and Rogue Feminists: The Origins of the Women's Shelter Movement in Canada,* implies.

McCarthy admits she had a hard time understanding the problems women were facing. "I was always independent and I always thought, 'Well, just get the hell out.'" When asked what changed her mind, she told this story:

"I had an experience with one lady who taught at the university, where her husband also taught. She was a nice lady. And for years, she was locked in her basement. And her husband would drive her to work and he would pick her up and drive her home, and then lock her in the basement again. And I couldn't believe this. I was driving her to court and she was telling me her story—it was such a shock. That's when I really woke up. She didn't have a single penny. That was the first time that I thought, 'Oh, here's somebody so well-educated and smart, who is in this situation.'"

---

2   Standing Committee on Health, Welfare and Social Affairs, *Wife Battering: Report on Violence in the Family,* 1980, https://parl.canadiana.ca/view/oop.com_HOC_3201_19_5/1.

Those moments of reckoning are still happening today. In 2014, professional football player Ray Rice—a two-hundred-pound NFL running back—was filmed striking his then-fiancée in an elevator after what appeared to be a brief argument. Janay Palmer Rice was flattened to the ground instantly. The couple married the next month; when video footage of the assault was released later that year, the hashtag #WhyIStayed began trending on Twitter. Writer Beverly Gooden, a domestic abuse survivor, started the hashtag, noting that people were zeroing in on why Janay Rice stayed with her husband, rather than why her husband had struck her with such force she was knocked unconscious.[3]

"We need to understand that violence against women and intimate partner violence is a complex issue and no one deserves or asks to be beaten," says Pat Vargas, who has served as executive director at A Safe Place in Sherwood Park, Alberta. "And if you stay in a relationship, there are many factors—and we shouldn't be asking why [the woman stayed]. Rather we should be asking, 'What support do we have in place for women who choose to live a life without violence?'"

❊ ❊ ❊

By 1973, women's groups across the country were fighting bureaucracies, stagnant social attitudes, and a lack of funds to open women's shelters. The first facilities specifically geared toward helping women escape domestic violence opened that year in Vancouver, Toronto, Langley, Saskatoon, and Calgary.

Lynn Zimmer, a young feminist behind the opening of Interval House in Toronto, told Goodhand, "Let's just say it was a spontaneous combustion thing and it just spread like wildfire. Because in our way, we each were the first, we didn't copy each other, we just did it."[4] Zimmer had posted an advertisement that read: "Want to do something for women in distress? If you're interested in forming a women's shelter, please come to this meeting." That gathering was held at a recently opened, federally funded feminist centre; the attendees included young university students, ready to attend protests and rally for feminist causes, and a handful of older women, some of whom had a personal understanding of the harms caused by domestic violence. They

---

3   Zosia Bielski, "A Simple Hashtag Reveals the Complexities Facing Women Who Experience Domestic Violence," *The Globe & Mail*, September 9, 2014.

4   Goodhand, *Runaway Wives and Rogue Feminists*, 52.

partnered with the city to find a rental and opened Interval House in January of that year.

On the other side of the country, in Langley, British Columbia, a small feminist group applied for federal government funding to open Ishtar Transition House, named for a mythical Mesopotamian goddess who represented love, war, justice, and power.[5] A three-hour drive south of Edmonton, Joyce Smith was leading the charge for the Calgary Women's Emergency Shelter. A mother and homemaker, Smith had gone back to school as a mature student to study social work and experienced an intense desire to change the lives of vulnerable women. "When other girls were talking about dirty diapers and a pot of coffee, Joyce and I talked about the welfare of the world and different things that were happening," a friend told the *Calgary Herald* in 2008, a year after Smith passed away.[6]

Feminist activists in Edmonton were building projects like the Rape Crisis Centre, which became a launchpad for many young workers who would go on to staff women's shelters as they opened in subsequent years across the province. The Edmonton chapter of the Catholic Women's League, made up of Beaudry and her friends, was hardly composed of young radicals, but their work still pushed social boundaries as they fought for resources for vulnerable women. Lynn Hannley, from the Edmonton Social Planning Council, worked beside them and says the group was initially driven by a sense of benevolence and charity. "But as they became engaged, it became an issue of rights. I was always impressed with them, to see how they evolved. I think it gave them strength to continue on."

But there were still blind spots, for the group and for society at large. The majority of clients who arrived at the storefront shelter run by EWS were Indigenous, landing in the city from reserves and settlements in northern Alberta. Groups such as the Métis Association of Alberta pushed for a new shelter, to be operated by an Indigenous board and staffed by people who knew Indigenous languages and were familiar with life on reserve.[7] It was an early example of how Indigenous women were ready and willing to tackle issues of violence and other social ills but struggled for resources and support for Indigenous-led solutions. It also showed how, since the very beginning, some of the main players in Alberta's women's shelter movement have had to

---

5   Ibid., 60.
6   Peter Green, "Joyce Smith," *Calgary Herald*, January 20, 2008, B5.
7   Proposal for Women's Interim Aid, Nagisayway peygamak (no date).

reckon with how to best meet the needs of Indigenous women—even if that meant stepping back—and to understand how Indigenous women's experiences with violence are entangled with racism, sexism, and colonialism.

After Edmonton's Women Shelter Ltd. decided to focus on opening a non-institutional home for women in crisis, specifically those fleeing domestic abuse, the organization spent months researching women's housing needs. Some members even corresponded with the staff of transition houses—as women's shelters were more commonly called at that time—in other parts of the country to learn more about their operations.[8] By 1978, the organization had produced a professional eleven-page proposal that outlined the need for a shelter for battered women. The document included a short scan of available services in Edmonton and a proposed outline of operations, including staffing levels and intake policies.

The women found a brown, four-suite, up-and-down apartment building that would become their shelter's first permanent home in the city's Beverly neighbourhood. The Clifford E. Lee Foundation purchased the building and then agreed to lease it to the shelter for one dollar per year, for ten years. Like every shelter in the 1970s, this one was filled with donated furniture, its renovations done by donated labour. Beaudry remembers the moment the foundation agreed to lease them the structure: "A dollar a year! Can you imagine what that was like? That was just an amazing thing."

The opening of WIN House was marked by an un-bylined article in the *Edmonton Journal* under the title, "Shelter for battered women opens."[9] The shelter's first executive director, the inimitable Ruth Pinkney, would become the public name and face of the shelter over the next decade. A registered psychiatric nurse, Pinkney would later tell a reporter that her job at WIN House involved overseeing budgets, counselling women in crisis, changing diapers, and washing dishes in a facility that had no dishwasher and a washing machine that had been broken since day one.[10]

She also had to educate the public about the dynamics of domestic violence, and the role of a women's shelter in helping women affected by it. "Our aim is not to break up marriages if there is any hope the husband can look at

---

8   Marsha Mildon, *WINning: The Trials, Tribulations, and Triumphs of Opening a Women's Shelter* (Edmonton: Housing for Women Book Society, 2020), 134.

9   "Shelter for Battered Women Opens," *Edmonton Journal*, December 6, 1978, B2.

10   Marta Gold, "Time for a Change, WIN House Director Says," *Edmonton Journal*, July 2, 1988, C11.

his behaviour and work to change it. . . . Sometimes it is best the women go back," Pinkney told a reporter in early 1979. "[But] many women go through repeated beatings and return to the husbands time and time again before they develop confidence that they can survive on their own."[11]

In less than a month, WIN House had served thirteen mothers and twenty-two children, according to a board report written by Ardis Beaudry in early 1979. The numbers continued to grow, and the women who had spent years fighting, fundraising, and advocating for a women's shelter knew their work wasn't done. "As soon as WIN House I was open, we knew we needed WIN House II," says Beaudry. "Because it was overflowing right off the bat." In September 1981, the group got city approval to construct a second shelter in Edmonton.

If the Edmonton shelter was quickly stretched to its limits, it follows that women in other parts of the province needed help, too. Domestic violence is not just an urban phenomenon, and in the 1980s and 1990s, women from smaller centres were ready to organize for the cause, too.

---

11   Wendy Koenig, "Price of Peace at Home May Be Too Costly," *Edmonton Journal*, January 4, 1979, B2.

A woman rests on a cot in an early shelter space in Edmonton in the 1970s. Lack of funding—and support in general—meant that women shared very confined quarters.

Material republished with the express permission of: Postmedia Network Inc. and the Provincial Archives of Alberta.

Prairie pragmatism drives the shelter movement

LENA

Lena Neufeld was on summer break from university in 1986 when her room-mate mentioned a job opening at the women's shelter in Lethbridge. Neufeld didn't know much about Harbour House, but figured it had to be better than delivering pizzas until 3 a.m. like she was doing at the time. She completed an application and was hired within a day.

The shelter occupied the top floor of Lethbridge's brick YWCA building on 8th Street. On her first day at work, Neufeld was buzzed up to the secure fourth floor; she stepped off the elevator and was almost immediately handed a box of Kleenex and told to speak to a woman waiting in the next room. The woman's husband had physically thrown her out of their home, and she had run to Harbour House for help.

"That was my training. I was told to just go in there and talk to her. I listened to her, but I think I was in a bit of shock. It was probably her first time at the shelter, so at least she didn't know what was supposed to happen and didn't recognize me for the newbie that I was," Neufeld remembers.

Neufeld grew up in Coaldale, a small town just a few kilometres outside of Lethbridge. She was thirty years old, divorced with two kids, and—although she didn't talk about it much—she knew what it was like to feel terror in the presence of her husband. For most of her marriage, Neufeld didn't recognize her husband's abuse for what it was. Then, when she experienced what she calls a "severe beating," she ran to her mother's house. "[My mother] told me, 'You can never go back because he will kill you.' I don't know how my mother knew to tell me that, but she must have seen something somewhere."

By the mid-1980s, the term "wife battering" was slowly creeping into the public's consciousness, even if none of Neufeld's friends were talking about it.

Harbour House had been established a few years before Neufeld arrived and was one of about a dozen shelters in Alberta in the early 1980s. After the first shelters opened in Calgary and Edmonton, the movement spread to smaller communities. The Lethbridge shelter was run under the organizational umbrella of the YWCA, as well as being housed there.

Neufeld remembers that Harbour House seemed chaotic when she arrived. There were twenty-eight beds and no executive to oversee the operation. Staff would usually work alone on twelve-hour shifts. Neufeld's official job title was Crisis Relief Counsellor, but while on shift she had to do the cooking, cleaning, intakes, office work, and one-on-one meetings. "You were responsible for everything. It was all your job," says Neufeld. She was paid $6.97 per hour.

Lethbridge is situated on Treaty 7 territory, and many of the shelter's clients came from nearby reserves, including the Kainai Nation and Piikani Nation. Neufeld recalls that many of the Indigenous women they served ended up returning to their home communities; there was less support in those days for women who wanted to start over. Indigenous women, especially, faced such barriers as discrimination from landlords when they tried to find housing—a problem that persists today. Meanwhile, family members and sometimes even clergy would show up at the shelter to talk to the women—both Indigenous and not—and quietly urge them to return to their families. "Because everybody wants mom to go back home, right?" says Neufeld.

The shelter often saw women with problems the staff simply weren't equipped to handle, even as training increased for shelter workers in later years. There was the woman who was convinced her body was being used to manufacture lightbulbs. There was the woman who showed up at Harbour House one night with a note pinned to the front of her dressing gown that read, "Take to Harbour House." Someone at the hospital had put the woman in a taxi and sent her over. Neufeld figures the woman either lived in YWCA housing on the bottom floors of the building, or hospital staff had decided that Harbour House would take her in since it operated 24/7.

"Back in the day, a lot of agencies used us as a dumping ground. They've got a problem client and they don't know what to do with her? They'll just say, 'Let's get her admitted to Harbour House.'" That kind of attitude persists even today.

Many women arrived with their children, and although shelters weren't initially designed to treat them as anything other than extra "heads on beds," it soon became apparent how deeply children were affected by domestic violence. Neufeld's colleague Kristine Cassie remembers one young boy who would check the doors and windows of the shelter every night to make sure they were locked. Then he'd take the fire extinguisher to bed with him. "His role should have been playing Lego and riding his bike. But he was the oldest of the kids so he was pseudo-mature for his young age and took on a role in the family as a protector." Other children, even toddlers, would swear at staff, mimicking the language they heard at home.

As chaotic as the job was, Neufeld immediately loved the work. The buzz of activity that characterized the day shift was replaced with relative calm after dark. Neufeld would sometimes stay up all night working on a puzzle with a client. Even if she knew a woman would return to a chaotic, violent home, she perceived small moments of change and reckoning. She remembers many women talking openly and eagerly, desperate to feel accepted and to be believed.

But the stories could also be traumatic for the listeners, and not everyone was cut out for the work. Cassie remembers the day an older woman came into the shelter with blood on her legs. She had been sexually assaulted in a condemned building across the street from the shelter. She just wanted to take a shower but staff tried to convince her to save her clothes and call the police. Two weeks later, she came back to thank the shelter staff for their help. Still, one staff member was traumatized by the entire incident. "She had never dealt with a sexual assault before and there's that feeling of powerlessness because you couldn't force the woman to go to the hospital or do anything else. But at least [the woman] knew she could come here," Cassie says.

A few years after Neufeld's arrival, there was a distinct turnover in shelter staff, and the newcomers seemed to represent a shift in both the profession and society's attitudes. Many of the newcomers were openly gay or self-described feminists, women whom Neufeld had never encountered in her life in and around Lethbridge. Some staff were willing to stretch the limits of their job descriptions. "If we saw a woman was really getting the shaft and there was no give, we'd have a little conference and we'd help get her things. She'd have a key and she'd have neighbours who would let us know when the husband was away. So, we'd go to the house to get what she needed. Some of my colleagues wanted to get militant and take spray paint and let the whole neighbourhood know what these men did. There was talk, but I don't think they ever did it."

That wasn't Neufeld's style. But she is still irked by newspaper obituaries in which a woman is described in loving terms by a husband who Neufeld knows inflicted pain and trauma on his wife when she was alive. She remembers one prominent political activist in southern Alberta whose wife spent many nights at the shelter, due to an unbearable life at home.

Almost forty years later, Neufeld says her shelter work was some of her best work. "It just felt so good to know that you had maybe made a difference. The people who come are so vulnerable. But sometimes you could just see them waking up and saying, 'Wow, this is happening to other people. It's not just me and I don't have to put up with this.'"

—*Lena Neufeld worked at Harbour House from 1986 to 1989. She went on to work in other positions with YWCA Lethbridge. She sometimes sees women who were once clients around town, and she continues to volunteer with Harbour House when she can.*

❧ ❧ ❧

There's a stubborn stereotype of rural Alberta as a bastion of conservatism. While it's true that the cities, towns, and hamlets outside of Edmonton and Calgary seem to perpetually vote conservative blue in elections, it can be harder to pinpoint the on-the-ground social values of the people who live there. After all, the province is full of contradictions. Alberta was home to the Famous Five that drove the Canadian suffragette movement. Albertans across the province still revere former Premier Peter Lougheed, a conservative who created a human rights commission and happily pumped money into the arts. Medicine Hat-born Doris Anderson was at the helm of *Chatelaine* magazine in the 1960s and 1970s, where she directed critical ink to abortion, sexuality, and child abuse when most mainstream Canadian publications would not.[1]

By 1982—the year male MPs in the House of Commons notoriously laughed at a female colleague's query about a report on domestic violence[2]— women's shelters had opened in a cluster of smaller Alberta cities: Medicine Hat, Fort McMurray, Grande Prairie, Cold Lake, and Lethbridge. These

---

1   Erin Collins, "Alberta's Dirty Little Progressive Secret," *CBC*, December 17, 2015.
2   Keri Sweetman, "Male MPs' Guffaws at Wife Beating Query Enrage Female MPs," *Ottawa Citizen*, May 13, 1982, 4.

shelters hadn't been established by government agencies, but by local citizens with limited funds and a conviction that women needed help.

Their challenges were often different from those of their big-city counterparts, as they had to convince funders that domestic violence wasn't just an urban phenomenon.[3] Decision-makers frequently assumed the problem wasn't widespread in their communities and that shelter beds devoted to women fleeing domestic abuse would sit empty. Or that what women in their communities actually needed was a crisis hotline. Or that perhaps a homeless shelter would serve more clientele. They were invariably wrong.

In 1986, Lisa Morgan went to work at the Dr. Margaret Savage Crisis Centre in Cold Lake. It's in an area known as "Lakeland," with hundreds of fish-filled lakes and farmland that stretches east to Saskatchewan. The town of Cold Lake is about a thirty-minute drive from Bonnyville and neighbours a Canadian Forces Base and the territories of the Cold Lake First Nations. The three communities are linked geographically and economically, but, at the time, they were unaware that they shared a common social problem: domestic violence.

"When I would do public education on the Base, people would say to me, 'Well, the people going to the Crisis Centre are from Cold Lake, the First Nation, and Bonnyville,'" Morgan remembers. Meanwhile, people from the Cold Lake First Nations thought the Centre was used by town residents and military personnel. And people from Bonnyville thought the Centre was only being used by their neighbours. "Nobody wanted to believe family violence was in their own backyard. It's the Indigenous people; it's the military people; it's the farmers. It's their culture, it's not ours."

One of the first tasks for any group trying to establish a women's shelter is to find a suitable space. In the 1980s, that usually meant any building with a kitchen and a few rooms that could house women and their children. Offices were set up in spare corners or sometimes even a garage. Shelter advocates looked for cheap or, even better, donated buildings. In Grande Prairie, a town councillor offered a small pink bungalow on Main Street. The original shelter in Cold Lake was a converted church with sturdy mesh coverings on the windows. The walls in the bedrooms didn't even go up to the ceiling. "We had bunk beds and we had kids bouncing from one bedroom to the next,"

---

3   Nancy Janovicek, *No Place to Go: Local Histories of the Battered Women's Shelter Movement* (Vancouver: UBC Press, 2007), 2.

recalls Morgan, who started out as a child support worker and spent most of her early years working from the kitchen since there was nowhere else to set up a desk.

In many towns, advocates had to fight neighbours who worried about plummeting property values if there were a shelter in their neighbourhood, or feared angry husbands roaming their streets. In Pincher Creek, it was racism, with some residents insisting the service would only be used by women from nearby First Nations. "I thought it would take maybe three years to open a women's shelter in Pincher Creek," says Wendy Ryan, who spent much longer than that advocating for a facility in the small southern Alberta town, as part of a local women's shelter steering committee. "When people told me it would take eight to ten years, I didn't believe them. But it was true."

One of the first facilities Ryan and her colleagues considered was an un-used nunnery just north of downtown. Ryan describes it as a "solid brick" structure, with about ten bedrooms, a shared kitchen facility, and plenty of bathrooms. In other words, it would have been perfect. Ryan says the build-ing had been inspected and her group had priced out the necessary renova-tions. But, at the last minute, the local priest flipped on his decision to offer them the building for just a few dollars, and they never received an adequate explanation why.

"Then we had a line on a fabulous house. It was a split house, so there was an apartment on the bottom and an apartment on top—there were two kitchens, two separate living quarters. But the neighbour across the street fought us," says Ryan. Town council rejected the application for the shelter after neighbours offered the familiar arguments about property values and crime. The first women's shelter in Pincher Creek eventually opened in a very small house on Main Street, and then moved to a medical clinic that was renovated for its new use.

Makeshift offices and improperly walled bedrooms aside, early shelters also had to improvise their approaches to security. In small towns, it was inevitable that the shelter's location would become known to anyone who really wanted to find out. Some facilities had fenced yards, but security fea-tures like cameras, double doors, intercoms, and bollards to prevent abusers from ramming their trucks through the front doors didn't become standard until many years later.

"There was one incident when I heard one of the ladies screaming around the time that everyone was going to bed," recalls Heather King, who started work at Croken House in Grande Prairie as a summer job during her break from college in 1981. "There was a great big drunk fellow pushing in the door and the women were pushing back on the door to shut it. And we were all pushing the door, saying, 'You have to leave! You have to leave!' And finally, I ran and called the police and they came and picked him up. So, security was not great. We didn't have good locks and there were so many ways to get into that facility."

But there wasn't enough money for proper security measures because there was barely enough to pay rent or meet payroll. In the fall of 1988, the Lurana Family Centre, an overflow facility run by an order of Franciscan sisters in Edmonton, closed temporarily due to a lack of funds. It was only after a weeks-long public awareness campaign aided by several prominent feminist organizations that the centre inked a new deal with the province. Overall, women's shelter budgets were shoestring and haphazard, with staff scrounging for donations and accepting outrageously low salaries for themselves. Shelters were finally becoming recognized as one of the most important interventions for women facing domestic abuse.[4] But the funding model was inadequate and unsustainable.

In the early 1980s, shelters were paid on a per-diem basis, receiving a set amount of money for every day a woman stayed. WIN House I in Edmonton, for example, received $5.50 per client, per day, from the department of social and community health in 1978.[5] Staff from Odyssey House in Grande Prairie remember being told in the early 1980s that their funding deal with the government was for 80 per cent of what the Edmonton shelters received, since they ran fewer programs. Individual shelters often had to negotiate their own agreements with local governments, creating disparities and uncertainty from organization to organization.

These funding models were particularly damaging to Indigenous women. Those who decided to leave their reserve could be caught in a dehumanizing fight among federal, provincial, and local social service agencies, each of which would argue that the women were not their responsibility and thus were not eligible for their help.[6] This type of dispute is similar to those meant

---

4   Linda MacLeod, *Wife Battering in Canada: The Vicious Cycle* (Hull: Canadian Government Publishing Centre, 1980), 48.

5   "Shelter for Battered Women Opens," *Edmonton Journal*, December 6, 1978, B2.

6   MacLeod, *Wife Battering in Canada*, 50.

to be addressed by Jordan's Principle,[7] which since 2016 has made strides toward resolving the jurisdictional breakdown in caring for Indigenous children in the healthcare system. A resolution to this problem for adult women would require adequate services on reserve as well as barrier-free access to off-reserve services. The first on-reserve shelters in Alberta, offering women from a handful of First Nations communities emergency accommodations on their own lands, didn't open until the 1990s.

The fight for sustained, equitable funding, so critical to women's shelters serving all types of clientele, was what prompted the formation of the Alberta Council of Women's Shelters (ACWS). At first, it was a loose coalition of shelter board chairs who knew they could better advocate if they made their demands in a single, strong voice. "The vision was to unite, and to get the government to recognize that shelters are a vital social service," says Loretta Bertol, the first provincial coordinator for ACWS. The per-diem funding scheme made long-term planning impossible and put tremendous strain on the women working to keep shelter doors open. They relied heavily on charitable donations for everything from table linens to food to beds. There was perennial uncertainty—and accompanying stress—about whether shelter workers would get their paycheques. Some shelter directors remember sleepless nights, thinking about staff who weren't being offered much money to begin with.

In Cold Lake, shelter director Joie Dery spent twenty years running a twenty-six-bed shelter even though she only received funding for eleven. Colleagues would later describe her as a "wizard" with a budget, her work "a testament to grit, perseverance, and to the fundamental principle of doing all that you can to keep women and children safe." Before the words "believe women" became an expression of the #MeToo movement, Dery lived that philosophy: she believed that women's stories should not be dismissed just because you couldn't always see their bruises. Dery, who passed away in 2011, retired just as the province agreed to fund a dozen more beds, meaning there would be more money for staff and supports at the shelter.

"When you look back at the archives of our budgets, it was just shameful. We were always running a deficit. But the organization took that on, women took that on," says Kristine Cassie, the former CEO of the YWCA Lethbridge

---

7   https://manitobachiefs.com/advocacy/jordans-principle/

and District. "I mean, there weren't eggs to fry up. You were living on next to nothing."

But as public awareness of domestic violence improved in the 1980s, so, too, did the funding. When, in 1982, men in the House of Commons laughed at NDP MP Margaret Mitchell's query about the need to help battered women, it was a dark but still illuminating moment. That elected politicians would snicker at a serious social issue was profoundly disappointing, but Mitchell ultimately used the incident to raise awareness of the problem. By the following year, the Criminal Code was amended to include marital rape as a crime. In Alberta, the government established the Office for the Prevention of Family Violence, the first of its kind in the country, in 1986. That office actively coordinated with the Alberta Council of Women's Shelters, and two years later, ACWS won its first major battle when the provincial government developed a standard contract for all off-reserve shelters. It was nothing short of a coup for the start-up coalition of women's shelters.

☿ ☿ ☿

The fight for funding has been enshrined in the shelter movement since its very beginning, but women also had to be formidable advocates and deft educators in order to garner public support for these facilities. For women in smaller communities, it sometimes meant walking a careful line to maintain social relationships with key community figures who could single-handedly determine whether or not a shelter would open.

In the 1980s, St. Paul residents Yvonne Caouette and Jean Quinn began holding meetings in a small office at the Mannawanis Friendship Centre to plan for a full-service shelter in their farming community. Caouette started working the town's Friday night bingos to fundraise for the project, and her family was soon recruited for the job, too. "There were fifty-two bingos a year, and we needed at least twelve volunteers a week." The Caouette family would have their kids and grandkids there. They'd walk around the floor and sell cards and markers. "I would tell the kids, 'If Alberta Gaming and Liquor comes and asks how old you are, you say: How old do I have to be to work here? That's how old I am.'" Decades later, the Caouette family was still working a handful of bingos every year.

Caouette made fundraising presentations to the most powerful networks in town, including business groups, the Knights of Columbus, and City Hall.

"The old mayor from St. Paul said, 'Well, I'd like you to bring me a picture of a battered woman.' A lot of them didn't believe it. It was women, too. I had a good friend from school who insulted me. She said, 'You people just do this to break up families.' I was so insulted." But Caouette persisted and, after years of advocacy, the Knights of Columbus offered some land for a shelter and $25,000. Then the St. Paul Lions Club kicked in $25,000, too. Caouette laughs, "I think people were so sick and tired of seeing us, they eventually said, 'Let's give them money to get rid of them!'" A new shelter finally opened in St. Paul in 1991.

Women like Caouette had to place themselves at the centre of small-town social life: the curling club, charity golf events, religious organizations. Women in small towns might come up against one skeptical gatekeeper with an undue amount of influence over charitable funds, says Nancy Janovicek, author of *No Place to Go: Local Histories of the Battered Women's Shelter Movement*. But they might also bump into the police chief at the grocery store, which could lead to a sit-down conversation about domestic abuse and the need for a women's shelter.

"These interpersonal relationships and those networks could hurt you, or they were an absolute asset—and they were often both at the same time. So, women networked," says Janovicek.

Despite their feats of diplomacy and networking, shelter advocates still faced widespread denial and pronouncements from public figures who scoffed at the issue outright. In 1986, the *Drumheller Mail* printed this item in its irreverent "Roundtable" column: "Did you know that November is Family Violence Prevention month, so don't beat up on your old lady in November, wait for December or January." The newspaper's publisher, Ossie Sheddy, refused to apologize in response to backlash from feminist and social service organizations. Instead, he wrote that "In thirty-five years, not one incident has been reported to the paper of such happenings."[8]

Even those who were on board for the generic cause of "helping women" often didn't want to see the issue "politicized", despite the fact that violence against women is inherently political, rooted in misogyny and abuse of power. This incongruity between the desire to help women in need, and a refusal to acknowledge the social forces that kept them in crisis, is perhaps best

---

8   Lorraine Locherty, "Violence 'Joke' Sparks Furore," *Calgary Herald*, December 17, 1988, B6.

highlighted by small-town Alberta's reaction to one word: feminism. Shelter workers and advocates may have strongly identified as feminists and with the feminist movement, but many realized that doing so publicly could actually hurt shelters as a whole. In other cases, the development of shelters was fueled more by a sense of Prairie pragmatism than by hot ideological conviction. In her book *State of Struggle*, Lois Harder argues that Alberta's women's shelters were spared "the full wrath of deficit cutting" that hit a lot of "special interest" organizations in the 1990s largely because shelters walked a fine line to avoid publicly linking feminism to the movement to prevent violence against women.[9]

But those forced to walk that line were inevitably put in an awkward position, required to soften the message that violence against women is a societal problem that calls for solutions geared specifically to the safety and well-being of women. Kristine Cassie, of Harbour House in Lethbridge, recalls being called a "man-hater" and being told that women's shelters weren't paying enough attention to male victims of abuse. "We recognize there are men who are abused, but the levels and the types of abuse are very different. It almost felt like you were apologizing for being a woman, that you were apologizing for focusing on women's needs and rights," she says.

Catherine Hedlin was executive director of the Medicine Hat Women's Shelter in 1989. Late that year, when a gunman walked into the École Polytechnique in Montreal, separated the men from the women, and opened fire, Hedlin was interviewed by the local newspaper about the national tragedy that left fourteen women dead. In the interview, she identified herself as a feminist. "My board was not happy," says Hedlin, who went on to become an associate professor at MacEwan University. "After my initial interview around the Montreal massacre, I rephrased my wording and took 'feminism' out because it made my community uncomfortable. When I talked about the massacre from that point on, I had to talk about it more as the actions of a man with mental illness. But I still wanted our community to understand that what happened in Montreal should never happen again. And that we need to look at issues of equality for men and women as one of the ways we address issues of violence. Whether or not we were acknowledging feminism, we were an organization that was trying to change the community for women. And if that meant not proclaiming my beliefs, I was willing to live with that."

---

9   Harder, *State of Struggle*, 128.

Hedlin clashed with her board on other fronts, too, including the amount of sick time shelter staff required. The board wanted to slash sick days in the middle of a fiscal year and Hedlin felt the decision revealed the board to be disconnected from the realities of the women who worked at and who stayed at the shelter. In Hedlin's observation, board members tended to be middle-class community members who didn't necessarily see the shelter as something they or their peers would use. Many clients who landed at the shelter were poor, with no other housing options available to them. Meanwhile, staff were being paid paltry salaries due to a lack of funding. Many had been drawn to the work because they, too, had experienced violence in their homes; for them, the work could be re-traumatizing. For others, like the worker at Harbour House who struggled after trying to help a sexual assault survivor, the cases they encountered could produce new trauma as the stories they heard time and time again affected their own mental well-being.

Hedlin herself was a private-school-educated woman who came into her position after having completed a master's degree. She lived in a different socio-economic realm than almost everyone else in the shelter, staff included. But at the time, no one was thinking much about how different life experiences could impact the work of keeping women safe. "We all came with very middle-class attitudes. Even the staff who weren't middle class measured things by middle-class standards—the idea of the Protestant work ethic, that success is about making a certain amount of money, that you'll marry and have kids, and if you have a career it will probably be in nursing or teaching. We expected that what our clients wanted would fall in line with those middle-class values."

The term "intersectionality"—the idea that combinations of race, class, sexuality, gender, ability, and other characteristics will affect a person's life experiences and how they are perceived and treated by others—was not coined until 1989, by American legal scholar Kimberlé Crenshaw. But to look back, it's obvious that the real-life experiences of many shelter clients, especially those who had lived in poverty, and Indigenous women, whose lives are inextricably affected by racism, sexism, economic exclusion, and colonialism, were affected by what we now understand as intersectionality, and are vastly different from the life experiences of many shelter leaders; their struggles against patriarchal norms would be different, too. Hedlin says that, at the time, "we were just starting to recognize that White middle class feminism was not the only version [of feminism]."

Others, however, were more familiar with that distinction. By the late 1980s, one woman from Siksika First Nation, near Calgary, had identified the chasm between second-wave White feminism, which had dominated the early phases of the shelter movement, and the realities of many shelter clients. And she was determined to do something about it.

Ruth Scalp Lock was working at a women's shelter in Calgary when she realized there was a gap in services for Indigenous women within the shelter system. She worked for years to secure funding and support for a shelter for Indigenous women in Calgary. The Native Women's Crisis Shelter, which would later become the Awo Taan Healing Lodge, opened in 1993 in Calgary.

Photo reproduced with permission from Jim Pritchard.

A shelter for Indigenous women

RUTH

My name is Ruth Scalp Lock. *Awo Taanaakii* is my Blackfoot name; it means Shield Woman. *Awo Taan* is a shield in my culture. My grandma gave me my name, and I respect it every day on my journey.[1]

I had a vision to start the Awo Taan Healing Lodge when I was working at a Calgary women's shelter in the 1980s. I was the only Native counsellor there. They didn't know how to work with our women, especially to fulfill their spiritual needs. There were no workshops, and Elders did not come to work with the women. In our life, if you don't have that spirituality, you're just like a shell. There's nothing in there.

One time I came to work and the counsellors were all anxious, excited, and concerned. I asked them, "What's going on here?" They thought a Native woman was smoking dope. So we went down to this woman's room and this Native woman was burning sweetgrass! When I would come back to work after days off, First Nations women would be waiting for me. I used to tell them, "See other counselors." But it takes trust, especially after all we've been through and how our spirits have been broken.

In my vision to start the shelter, I dreamt about a man. We were walking down a road together and he had a long, white beard. Little did I know he was a retired professor from the University of Calgary. His name was Nelson Gutnick, and he did a lot of good work with us Natives in Calgary. Indian Affairs used to put our women at the York Hotel, right on skid row, and these women had to wait until there was space at the shelters. Nelson was always concerned about our women, and he went out of his way to help them. Any time I had a question or if I was having a hard time, he always supported me.

---

[1] This story is based on several interviews with Ruth Scalp Lock. The text has been condensed and lightly edited for clarity.

He was like a father and a mentor. I'm a recovering alcoholic of forty-two years sobriety, and when I was having a hard time, he told me, "Ruth, you're going to get your life together and you're going to be doing something for your people."

When I met with the director of my shelter, I told her, "'I know you do your best to fulfill the needs of Native women, but we strongly need our own shelter. I'm not working behind anybody's back, I'm not that kind of person." I approached Alvin Manitopyes, with the Secretary of State Department, for funding to do a needs assessment. It stipulated that we should have our own shelter. Then we hired Gerri Many Fingers, and she really ran with the whole thing. We finally got our board established, we got our charitable number, and we had an office at the Native Friendship Centre.

My feeling to help women is there for a number of reasons. I had a sister who was murdered. I have a cousin who has been missing since 1961 in Saskatchewan. I had a very good friend from Hobbema[2] who was found dead in her basement here in Calgary one summer. Her case was closed by the Calgary police. All these things push me. I just finished talking to my niece and I told her: "The whole intent behind Awo Taan goes way back. This is not a new thing for me." And when you have it in your heart to help people, you keep going. It might take a long time. It took at least eight years to really get the shelter going.

I felt so many of my people did not support me because they don't want to say, "This is the truth. This is what's happening to our women." There were all these put-downs by the men and sometimes even the women in my community. They would say: "I can't even give a dirty look to my wife anymore, she goes running to Ruth and Ruth takes her to a shelter." There's still denial.

There were so many feminist women who put me down, too. My vision was that we would work with men, too. I held my ground and I told them, "If I didn't like men, then I wouldn't like my father or my grandfather." My values are so different from some young women. I didn't like a lot of men either, especially the Catholic priests for the sexual abuse that I went through in my community. When I was applying to work at the shelter in Calgary, I thought I had dealt with a lot of my stuff; but no, I hadn't. When the women started to disclose sexual abuse to me, I couldn't take it. I cried deep inside and I went

---

2   Hobbema, Alberta, was renamed Maskwacis in 2014; it is the community representing the Ermineskin Cree Nation, the Louis Bull Tribe, Montana First Nation, and the Samson Cree Nation.

to a psychologist. "Help me with the sexual abuse," I said. Where would I be today if I hadn't?

I told these young women that I can understand where they're coming from, but it doesn't work that way with me or my culture. All my brothers were survivors of residential school. Where are they today? They're six feet under. They never had the opportunity to deal with the sexual abuse they experienced at the residential school. These issues are so deep-rooted. And where do men go to talk about these issues? They end up in court. One of my jobs is to attend court at the Siksika First Nation, and last week our court docket was eighteen pages long. The week before, it was twenty-two pages. There are men charged with sexual assault, rape, domestic violence. I know I have to look at the men. They need help, too.

Sometimes I would let go of all of my shelter work for a month, two months because it was so frustrating. We went to community meetings all over the city. We would have community meetings in the rich areas and, oh my gosh! There was so much prejudice and so many racial remarks. "What are we going to do if your drunken men are looking for women on our streets?" they said. They didn't want us to build a shelter there.

Then one time, the city was going to let us build a house in an industrial area in Calgary. I said, "No way! We don't belong there." I was so ticked off. I got up and I said, "Thank you, Mayor. Thank you, Council. You might as well put us in the Calgary Zoo, if that's how you think of us!" There's no way we were going to go to these places. You're going to have to give your head a really good shake and wake up.

There was so much negotiating. We worked with Ralph Klein, and then we finally got our building.

My grandma gave me the name *Awo Taanaakii* when we opened the shelter. My name is the outcome of my walk and being sober. I always have to think of my grandma who watched me on my walk. She told me, "One day, you're going to get your rewards for helping these women." She could have given the name to any one of her granddaughters, but she gave it to me.

My son and my nephews sang at the opening of Awo Taan. My son was telling me the other day, "I still remember that song, Mom. It was so spiritual." He said that the women, when they come through the shelter, they're going to be protected. There's so much sacredness to this place.

I've now passed on the name *Awo Taanaakii* to my great-granddaughter. In Siksika, some of us have four names. Beaver Woman is my third name, and I'll get my fourth name when I get to the spirit world. My grandmother told me that I would have to transfer my name at some point. To me it's so important, it has to be carried on. When teachings are shared with you, when Elders tell you to do something, you have to follow through.

—*Ruth Scalp Lock is a member of the Siksika Nation, which is part of the Blackfoot Confederacy, near Calgary. She is the author of* My Name Is Shield Woman: A Hard Road to Healing, Vision, and Leadership *(2014). Scalp Lock's work led to the establishment of the first off-reserve shelter for Indigenous women in Alberta. The Native Women's Crisis Shelter, which would later become the Awo Taan Healing Lodge, opened March 10, 1993, in Calgary. Awo Taan was a member of the Alberta Council of Women's Shelters from 1993 to 2014.*

꙰ ꙰ ꙰

Imagine a circle of children seated around a fire. They are the most important members of a community and therefore positioned near the warmth of the flames. Now, imagine a ring of women, those who give and sustain life, encircling the children. The women are surrounded by the community's Elders, who share their knowledge and wisdom. Finally, those standing in the outermost circle are men—protectors and hunters—who stand with their backs to the elements.

Janet Gladue, a member of the Bigstone Cree Nation in northern Alberta and former executive director of the Nation's Neepinise Family Healing Centre, presented this concept of community and family at a 2006 women's shelter conference in Mexico City. Gladue explained to the participants from Central and South America how, in Canada, colonization and the arrival of settlers destroyed the circles. "They said, 'Let's put your kids in school.' They took away all of the children. Right then, when they started taking away the children, the nest was empty. There was nothing in there. There was nothing to live for. The circle was disrupted."

Ongoing colonization affects every facet of life in Canada, and women's shelters are no exception. About 60 per cent of Indigenous women in Canada report having experienced some form of intimate partner violence in their lives, compared to 44 per cent of non-Indigenous women, according to a

2018 national survey.[3] Indigenous women are almost twice as likely to have survived physical or sexual violence, with 44 per cent of Indigenous women reporting such experiences compared to 25 per cent of other women. And Indigenous women are more than three times as likely to have experienced extreme violence, such as choking, beating, or threats with a weapon, compared to other women.

It's a lived reality that has been well documented by Indigenous organizations across Canada for decades: "It is not possible to find a First Nations or Métis woman . . . whose life has not been affected in some way by family violence. Either as a child witnessing spousal assault, as a child victim herself, as an adult victim of a husband or boyfriend's violence, or as a grandmother who witnesses the physical and emotional scars of her daughter or her granddaughter's beatings; we are all victims of violent family situations and we want it stop now," wrote the Ontario Native Women's Association (ONWA) in its seminal 1989 report, *Breaking Free: A Proposal for Change to Aboriginal Family Violence.*[4]

In the preface to its report, the ONWA identifies the root causes of this extensive violence: racial prejudice and the Indian Act, which have created poor socio-economic conditions for Indigenous people across the country. But the harm goes beyond the effects of poverty: intergenerational trauma and cycles of abuse that stem from loss of connection to the land, loss of ceremony and language, and disruption of the family that accompanied colonization and manifested as addictions and violence, are also the result of this legislation.

The Indian Act has always been particularly harmful to First Nations women. Written in 1876, it reflects the odious characterizations of Indigenous women that were created by early colonizers of Canada: they were uncivilized, a menace, prostitutes. "This made it easy for early police misconduct (including rape and murder) to go relatively unpunished," according to the executive summary of the final report from the National Inquiry Into Missing

---

3   Loanna Heidinger, *Intimate Partner Violence: Experiences of First Nation, Métis and Inuit Women in Canada* (Canadian Centre for Justice and Community Statistics, 2018), https://www150.statcan.gc.ca/n1/en/pub/85-002-x/2021001/article/00007-eng.pdf?st=rnnvytbZ, 4-5.

4   *A Proposal for Change to Aboriginal Family Violence* (Ontario Native Women's Association, 1989) iii.

and Murdered Indigenous Women and Girls.[5] That same dehumanizing indifference persists today; the families and friends of missing and murdered Indigenous women say police regularly don't take their cases seriously or victim-blame those who have been hurt, causing many not to approach the police at all, even in the face of violence.

The Indian Act contributed to dehumanizing attitudes toward First Nations women, in part, by imposing patriarchal structures on Indigenous communities, many of which had been previously organized along matrilineal lines. The Act denied First Nations women full participation in band democracy, and, perhaps most harmful, it defined a woman's humanity only in relation to a man. First Nations women who married non-status or non-First Nations men lost their own Indian status, Treaty benefits, and the right to live on their reserves, as did their children. It was a sexist piece of legislation that restricted the right of First Nations women to choose whom to marry, with whom to have children, and where to live. It affected the most intimate decisions of a woman's life.

"I received a letter from Indian and Northern Affairs that said, no question, no choice on my part, that I was no longer a member of my community and [they] gave me a cheque for $35," Jeannette Corbiere Lavell, from the Wikwemikong First Nation in Ontario, told a newspaper about what happened when she married a non-Indigenous man in 1970.[6]

Corbiere Lavell, who would become a founding member of the Ontario Native Women's Association, challenged the Act all the way to the Supreme Court of Canada, which rejected her case in 1973. Other First Nations groups, such as the Alberta-based Indian Rights for Indian Women, were also fighting for change, often coming up against Indigenous male leaders who saw this fight as a threat to their own leadership and perceived any changes to the Indian Act as a potential pretext for the government to abolish Indian status altogether.[7] First Nations women faced stiff opposition within their own communities, leading to confrontation, division, and sometimes ostracization. Other women, like Yvonne Bédard and now-Senator Sandra Lovelace Nicholas, took the cause to court, drawing critical public attention to the

---

5   *Executive Summary of the Final Report, National Inquiry Into Missing and Murdered Indigenous Women and Girls*, 17.

6   Rick Garrett, "Order of Canada Recipients Well-Deserving," *Anishinabek News*, January 5, 2018.

7   Rebick, *Ten Thousand Roses*, 108.

sexism and unfairness of the legislation. It wasn't until the Charter of Rights and Freedom was proclaimed that in 1985 this section of the Act was repealed.

But the Indian Act had already severed the ties of many First Nations women to their communities—physical, cultural, and familial. Women were not only cut off from their reserves but also from the systems of support there, leaving them more vulnerable to economic hardship and social harms, including domestic violence. The National Inquiry heard that, "without access to their own ways of living on traditional territories, which includes supporting others in times of hardship, many families and survivors [spoke] about their struggles with poverty, homelessness, addiction, and other challenges—struggles that were often greatly compounded by the lack of access to familiar, community, and cultural support."[8]

Just as harmful and traumatic for Indigenous women was Canada's residential school system, which saw Indigenous children removed from their parents' homes to be taught in church-run schools where the goal was to "take the Indian out of the child." The system devastated tight-knit Indigenous family and community structures—a form of family violence in itself, argues Mohawk lawyer and author Patricia Monture-Angus.[9] Children—boys and girls alike—frequently faced emotional, physical, and sexual abuse in the schools, which made them easier targets for abuse later in life, and more likely to perpetuate cycles of abuse. For many, violence was normalized, especially when people in positions of trust did not provide the help these children needed. According to the National Inquiry, "The normalization of violence within this context has serious repercussions in terms of Indigenous women's ability to protect themselves when it is necessary to do so. In many of the truths shared by witnesses, the normalization of violence could be traced back through family lines to trauma experienced in residential and day schools, to the Sixties Scoop, and to other forms of colonial violence."[10] (The Sixties Scoop is a term coined in 1983 by Patrick Johnson, author of *Native Children and the Child Welfare System*, and refers to a period in the mid-1900s when Indigenous children were taken, en masse, from their families and placed

---

8   *Executive Summary of the Final Report, National Inquiry Into Missing and Murdered Indigenous Women and Girls*, 24.

9   Janovicek, *No Place to Go*, 12.

10   *Executive Summary of the Final Report, National Inquiry Into Missing and Murdered Indigenous Women and Girls*, 33.

in the child welfare system, often without the consent of their families or bands.[11])

The children who were abused and un-parented in residential schools often grew into adults who were hurt, angry, unhealed, and did not themselves know how to parent or maintain healthy relationships. As Janet Gladue remembers about the disruption of the family circle, "There was nothing to live for. That's where the destruction came."

The National Inquiry into Missing and Murdered Indigenous Women and Girls found that Indigenous women, girls, and LGBTQ2SIA+ people in this country are the victims of a "Canadian genocide." It is a striking indictment of how their lives are at risk, in their own homes and within society at large.

🌿 🌿 🌿

As women's shelters opened across the country in the 1980s and 1990s, they were established as safe spaces for all women seeking help to escape domestic violence. But the systemic racism against Indigenous people in Canada would inevitably affect how Indigenous women could access these services.

Indigenous women who entered shelters would usually find they were run by boards and staff that were mostly—if not entirely—composed of White women. Did they understand the consequences Indigenous women faced if they left their home communities? Did they understand Indigenous languages and cultures? Did they understand the systemic racism that Indigenous women experienced every day in their lives?

"When I first came into a shelter in the city [from my reserve], I felt confused. I tried to explain my feelings but nobody understood," said Marilyn Fraser-King at the opening of the Native Women's Crisis Shelter, which would later become Awo Taan. Fraser-King was a board member of the organization. "I couldn't just go and do what they asked of me. I didn't have a car. I didn't have a phone. I had no neighbours."[12]

June Wiggins worked with Ruth Scalp Lock at Sheriff King Home, a women's shelter opened by the YWCA in Calgary in 1983. Scalp Lock had set up an Indigenous women's group, which operated through the shelter's

---

11 https://indigenousfoundations.arts.ubc.ca/sixties_scoop/
12 Eva Ferguson, "Out from the Shadows," *Calgary Herald,* March 11, 1993, B1.

outreach program, and Wiggins participated in the meetings as part of her work toward a master's degree. She recounted her experiences in Scalp Lock's book, *My Name is Shield Woman*.

> When we did groups with the Natives and the White women, it didn't go over well, because the Native women were very quiet. It was really evident at the shelter too that the Aboriginal women . . . were very careful which staff could relate to them culturally.

> But when [Native] women had their own group, they were very vocal. The stories they told were incredible. A lot of them related back to residential schools. I remember one group talking about women going missing on the reserves. It was almost every one of them had an aunt or a cousin that they had never heard from again. They talked a lot about what it was like in residential school, and it was amazing how they helped each other. The older kids helped the younger ones to learn to speak English just to get by. That was the big thing.

> There was a need to understand cultural issues or why they were doing things differently. For example, they take on [their] kids. It could be the sister's kid, but they'll take the kid and that'll be their kid, but it's really not their kid. So, you can get a woman that shows up with seven or eight kids, but she's only twenty-four, and she says they're all her kids. So it's this whole thing of family. . . . I think Ruth basically educated all the counsellors on a lot of First Nations issues.[13]

Wiggins's account highlights what many women working in shelters didn't know about Indigenous kinship connections and the effects of intergenerational trauma on their Indigenous clients. At the same time, her observations point to how the experiences of Indigenous women were often best articulated in a safe environment with others who had gone through similar events in their lives. Wiggins said that Scalp Lock educated herself and others not only on the issues Indigenous women faced, but also on the need for a shelter to specifically serve this population in Alberta.

---

13   Ruth Scalp Lock and Jim Pritchard, *My Name Is Shield Woman: A Hard Road to Healing, Vision, and Leadership* (Day Time Moon, 2014), 87.

In the early 1990s, a handful of shelters opened on First Nations reserves in Alberta, after the federal government opened a stream of funding for these facilities. (The story of Alberta's on-reserve shelters is covered in more detail in Chapter 7.) In Calgary, it took years of lobbying by Ruth Scalp Lock, and colleagues like Marilyn Fraser-King and Gerri Many Fingers, before the Native Women's Crisis Shelter opened in a temporary location on March 10, 1993. It was geared toward Indigenous women, but women of all ethnicities could use their services. Awo Taan, the permanent, $1.5-million, twenty-four-bed location, opened two years later, funded primarily by private donations and a provincial government loan guarantee.

Scalp Lock credits former Premier Ralph Klein for financially securing the development of Awo Taan. Perhaps unexpected for a White, conservative Alberta premier who focused on cost-cutting above all else, Klein had a strong relationship with many members of the Siksika Nation. The closeness dated back to his reporter days in the 1970s when he produced a documentary about poor living conditions on the reserve, a situation that clearly shook him. He was adopted into the Siksika Blackfoot Nation in 1993, and Scalp Lock referred to Klein as her "brother": "One day, when he was the premier, he sat down with his caucus and he said this to the table: 'From this day forward, all of you, you're going to start funding my sister's shelter.'"

Gerri Many Fingers served as Awo Taan's first director. She told a reporter in 1994 that she would often sit with the women who came there. "I talk to them about issues of race, discrimination, the politics of the system; and I tell them because they are women, because they are single, because they are Native, they will face all of these. But in order to start the process of healing, they have to find self-esteem and create a strong network of support around themselves."[14]

Looking back now, many White women who were part of the early shelter movement express essentially the same sentiment when reflecting on the specific circumstances of Indigenous women who were fighting or fleeing domestic violence: *we didn't know what we didn't know.* They acknowledge that the gatekeepers and celebrated trailblazers of the movement at the time were often ignorant of the extent to which race and gender overlap to shape the experiences of women in this country. "Indian women face obstacles in their struggles for change that the White middle class women's movement

---

14   "Gerri Many Fingers Community Service," *Calgary Herald*, June 19, 1994, B5.

has never had to deal with," said Karen Fish, a member of the BC Indian Homemakers' Association in 1977. "Indian women are discriminated against because they are Indian, because they are women, and more than either of these, they are discriminated against because they are Indian women."[15]

For Indigenous women like Ruth Scalp Lock, the fight against family violence had to be holistic, and had to include offering help to men who abuse their partners. Whereas the mainstream shelter movement posited that family violence is rooted in patriarchal power structures, the Indigenous perspective sees the root cause as the colonial disruption of the family. While both Indigenous and mainstream feminists want to end violence against women, they diverge on one of the core tenets of the women's shelter movement, which has been to urge institutions like the police and politicians to treat domestic violence as a crime and not merely a family affair.

"Feminists challenged the dominant social view that women provoked men's violence and that it was better for the family if abused women tried to make their marriages work," writes Nancy Janovicek. "Aboriginal activists also developed theories of violence that conceptualized it as a social rather than an individual problem, but the programs that Aboriginal women developed sought to strengthen the family and provide services for all members of violent families, including the abusers."[16]

To Scalp Lock, it appeared that young, White feminists hated men. It was her gut reaction to two different approaches to the causes—and cures—of domestic violence against women. While everyone agrees that keeping women physically safe is the top priority, there are divergent views on what the rest of the fight against domestic violence should look like. Scalp Lock viewed men in prison as victims, too. She could see the over-representation of Indigenous men in the country's criminal justice system and felt that sending more of her brothers, cousins, uncles, and neighbours into that system—without access to counselling or treatment—would only fuel a cycle of alienation from culture and broken family relations that led to violence in the first place. Locking someone up within a colonial institution that was never designed for healing Indigenous trauma would do nothing to help restore the circle of relations.

15   Sarah A. Nickel, "I Am Not a Women's Libber, Although Sometimes I Sound Like One: Indigenous Feminism and Politicized Motherhood," *The American Indian Quarterly* 41, no. 4 (Fall 2017).

16   Janovicek, *No Place to Go*, 3.

There are still more reasons that Scalp Lock and others like her would resist involving the criminal justice system in resolving problems of family violence. Indigenous communities, and other racialized communities, are disproportionately victims of police violence itself, which further reinforces the view that the police may not be part of the solution to these problems. Further, "[t]he emphasis on the criminalization of domestic violence has been far less effective for Aboriginal women, immigrant women and women of colour who rely on strong connections to their communities to counter racism and exclusion from Canadian society," Janovicek writes. "Women from these social groups are often reluctant to involve the police because they do not want to draw negative attention to their communities, or face censure from community leaders if they do."[17]

Scalp Lock says her vision was summarily dismissed by some in Alberta's shelter movement in the early 1990s, even if working with the whole family unit was always the intent of Awo Taan. Over time, more and more programs were developed to focus on or include work with men, such as *Oskâyi Kiskinotahn*, which ran out of Sheriff King Home, or Walking the Path Together, which was developed by on-reserve shelters and the Alberta Council of Women's Shelters and included opportunities for Indigenous men to find a new path in their family relations. Eventually, programming for men also became a part of mainstream shelter programming, although never without controversy or questions about its efficacy.[18] (The topic of men's programming will be returned to in Chapter 5.)

Oskâyi Kiskinotahn began as part of the regular men's group programming that was run out of the YWCA's Sheriff King Home in Calgary. By the late 1990s, facilitators had observed that many of the men's group participants were Indigenous, and that their needs were not being met by mainstream men's programming. Sheriff King and Awo Taan—led by Strengthening the Spirit, a subcommittee of the Action Committee Against Violence—worked with Elders to develop a more culturally appropriate program. The name *Oskâyi Kiskinotahn* (New Directions) was gifted by Olive Manitopyes, a well-known and beloved Cree Elder in the community who worked for years at Sheriff King Home and Awo Taan. The program was designed to reduce the incidence of domestic violence in families and ultimately included

---

17   Ibid., 14.
18   Intimate Partner Violence: Systematic Review Summary

programming designed for men, women, and children to discuss topics such as colonization, intergenerational trauma, residential schools, cultural identity, and healing. The men's and women's programming continues today and is now run out of several locations, including the Calgary Correctional Centre, the Siksika Nation, and Tsuut'ina Nation.

In other shelters, White women like Brenda Brochu were starting to wake up to the realities faced by Indigenous women, and they began integrating support for the latter into the very core of the work they did. Brochu, who helped to start the first women's shelter in Grande Prairie in 1980, moved to the Peace River area in the 1990s. There, she worked part-time in the local jail and part-time as a crisis intervention worker at the Peace River Regional Women's Shelter. At the shelter, she saw disproportionate numbers of Indigenous women seeking help. Then she started noticing news stories about women who had died or gone missing. She clipped articles out of the newspaper any time she saw a case—and soon realized most of the women involved were Indigenous.

When Brochu became director of the shelter in 1998, she aimed for half her staff to be Indigenous. She funded staff to attend Indigenous-run retreats that focused on awareness of history and culture. Smudging was permitted at the shelter and, she says, "It was even important in the decor and the artwork to have pictures that Aboriginal people could relate to. It couldn't only be that way, because everyone had to be comfortable there, but we didn't want to make the shelter an alien experience for Aboriginal women."

In 2004, Brochu received an email from the Native Women's Association of Canada, inviting the shelter to take part in a Sisters in Spirit project to remember Indigenous women who had gone missing or been murdered. She was a member of the town's Aboriginal Interagency Committee at the time, so she took the proposal to the group. The response was tremendous, and Indigenous groups laid the groundwork for a memorial based on activism, tradition, and remembrance. Brochu still remembers the number of women who attended the memorial. It crystallized for her just how acute the crisis of missing and murdered women was for Indigenous women in her community.

Her work was a sign of how shelters were developing their approaches to survivors, and to their greater activism.

By the 1990s, women's shelters in Alberta had moved past the stage of scrounging for the basics, like donated buildings and meagre salaries for a skeleton staff. People like Ruth Scalp Lock, Gerri Many Fingers, and Brenda

Brochu were pushing Alberta's women's shelters to think of new and better ways of operating. Perhaps nowhere was that more evident than in Calgary. The city was growing steadily by the second half of the decade, pushing towards a population of one million. Among those residents was a dynamic cadre of women who wanted to change the world of women's shelters by piloting new programs and connecting with others—even conservative politicians like Ralph Klein—to make it happen.

A woman sleeps on a cushion on the floor in Edmonton in the 1970s.

Calgary, fired up for change

ANITA

Anita's escape from her marriage began at her daughter's preschool. There had been another argument with her husband, this time in the car as they drove to pick up their child. Anita was crying when she walked into the Calgary church where the preschool was housed, and she asked to see the pastor. She told him her story.

They prayed for a few minutes and the pastor told Anita that a church member worked at a women's shelter in the city. He would arrange for the woman to meet Anita the next time she dropped off her daughter.

Anita, who grew up in Malaysia, remembers replying, "What is a shelter? I don't want to go there."

Anita had met her Canadian husband, "Brian,"[1] through a friend and their relationship blossomed online before they were able to meet in person. She came from a conservative Christian family; her parents had always told her to avoid men who smoked, drank, or partied too much. Her husband-to-be did none of those things, and she imagined they would start their new lives together on the other side of the world. She was thirty-two when they married.

Anita arrived in Canada in August 2005. She knew no one, other than her husband, and it was soon apparent he wanted to keep it that way. He answered the phone if it rang and answered the door if someone knocked. Anita was isolated and living with an increasingly abusive man who hit her for things like losing a pen or not eating all of the groceries he bought. When she got pregnant, Brian told her to abort the child or he would have her deported. Anita refused.

---

1   Brian is not Anita's husband's real name.

By 2006, with a small baby in the house and another on the way, the family moved to Calgary, where Brian was preparing to take a pilot training program. They bounced between houses and apartments because Brian repeatedly got into fights with neighbours and landlords. Inside their home, the beatings and the violence were getting worse. One day, Brian pressed a knife into Anita's back when she tried to escape the house to call for help. At night, Anita slept with her children on either side of her, while her husband stayed in a different room. She grasped a knife in one hand and a cell phone in the other. She kept the phone under her pillow and trained her hand to memorize the motions needed to dial 911.

"Sometimes I'd think, 'This is the night I'll be fighting for my life.' I had one of those Nokia phones, with the numbers that you press. I remembered where to press my fingers for 911. . . . '911. 911. 911.' The number was ringing in my head all the time."

At the church-based preschool, the pastor followed through on his promise and brought a caseworker to the church the following week. Anita again asked, "What is a shelter?" The caseworker described it to her as a safe place for women and children to stay until they find a place to live. They met again in the following weeks, devising a plan for Anita to leave. At the time, her husband was being held in a psychiatric hospital for an assessment following another fight with a neighbour and a subsequent court appearance during which he swore and insulted the judge. Anita knew she had just a few weeks before he'd be released, so she had to make a move before that happened.

The caseworker called the YWCA Sheriff King Home in Calgary to tell them about Anita. Then she gave Anita a day and time to leave. It didn't go as smoothly as everyone had hoped. Calgary was a city of sprawling suburbs. It's possible to spend your whole life in your own quadrant, driving between strip malls for daily errands, never entering the downtown core. Anita barely knew how to find the grocery store in her own neighbourhood, let alone a building in an unfamiliar part of town. "She gave me the address but I didn't know where to go. I was driving around and around and I couldn't find the place. I called them and they didn't understand me and I didn't understand them. I almost went back to my house. It took me almost two hours to find the place, with my GPS and my broken English," Anita remembers.

The first days were difficult and disorienting. Sheriff King Home was so different from what she was expecting, she almost thought she had been taken to jail. Part of the problem, she says now, was that she truly had no idea what a shelter was, even after it was described to her. She didn't like the shared living spaces—she says she has an obsession with cleanliness—and felt she couldn't trust how it had been cleaned. But when her husband showed up at Sheriff King Home and told staff he wanted to see his wife, she knew there was no going back. "If I go home, he will kill me," she remembers thinking. The staff told him to leave before they called the police.

A week later, a space opened at Discovery House, a second-stage shelter in Calgary where women can stay for longer terms to get on their feet and figure out things like work, legal issues, and their own mental well-being. There, Anita and her now two children had their own small apartment, with a kitchen and bedroom. She finally started to feel comfortable about leaving her home, although her husband was still always present in her thoughts. She looked up the address for every police station in Calgary so that if she saw him on the street, she would know where to go. She still slept with a knife in one hand and a cell phone in the other.

At Discovery House, Anita made her first Canadian friends—women who had also left abusive marriages. One woman was originally from China, the other from Kyrgyzstan. There was some relief in knowing other women had experienced similar situations, and that she wasn't the only one. There was relief in knowing she had friends she could count on for help.

But Anita thinks that, even at that time, there wasn't enough support for immigrant women in the shelter system. Calgary was among the province's shelters that had begun developing programming, outreach, and publications in various languages to support women from the city's growing immigrant communities. It was a formidable effort, but, on the ground, Anita still felt like she didn't know how to access all the help she needed.

"I was coming from a different culture, and my expectations were different. I was hoping someone would say, 'Let me hold your hand and we'll do this or we'll do that.' But from the workers' perspective, they had to go by the book and the policies they have in place. I know they're trying to teach women to be independent, but if you're not born here and you don't know the system or the resources available, you still need people to tell you what to do and where to go. They should connect them right away with cultural brokers."

Anita often took her children to the public library, where she'd pick up pamphlets for various programs around the city. She'd Google any program with the word "immigrant" in the title and soon found her way to ESL classes. She took an employment skills training class and then signed up with a temp agency that helped her land her first job. She eventually moved out of Discovery House and into a townhouse owned by the Calgary Housing Company.

But she didn't leave the shelter system forever. Her husband stalked her. When things felt particularly dangerous, she would go back to one of the shelters in the city. If they were full, she'd drive to shelters as far away as Strathmore or even Brooks, an hour or two out of town. When her husband demanded visits with the children, she went back to the YWCA Sheriff King Home's Safe Visitation Centre, where staff were available to supervise court-ordered visits with non-custodial parents.

Almost a decade after her first night at Sheriff King Home, Anita now has a job at another shelter in Calgary. "Every time I see new clients moving in, I feel I have a connection with each of them. I'm not a social worker, but somehow I always have a connection with them, especially with immigrants. I always try to help them."

—Anita lives in the Calgary area with her two children. She asked that her last name not be used to protect her children's privacy and for her own safety.

※ ※ ※

When Anita arrived in Calgary in 2006, the city was booming. Real estate prices were soaring, construction cranes were a fixture in the downtown core, and people were moving there from across the country, drawn by jobs that were fueled by oil prices hurtling toward US$100 per barrel. It was a quintessential boom period in a city that's long been defined by cycles of boom and bust. There's a certain confidence that comes from those heady times of economic expansion, and, partnered with a western frontier mythology, it makes for a city ethos of free thinking and risk-taking, even when the economy isn't in overdrive, and even outside the private sector. Women's shelters in Calgary have always embodied that boldness of spirit.

The Calgary Women's Emergency Shelter (CWES) opened in 1973, making it one of the first such facilities in the country. Its foundation story is rooted in the same feminist activism that propelled the opening of similar shelters across Canada. Joyce Smith, one of the pioneering founders of CWES, was a stay-at-home mom who went back to school at the age of thirty-six to study social work at the University of Calgary; there, she completed her practicum at a fledgling shelter for transient people, called Oasis.[2] She was still at Oasis in 1973 when the shelter narrowed its focus to helping abused women, and soon after she was named director of CWES. Smith, who died in 2007, was described by her sister as a driven woman with a social conscience, who "didn't lack for guts or courage."[3]

CWES started out in a three-storey house in the city's Beltline neighbourhood, on the edge of downtown. In the early years, women slept in donated bunk beds and were responsible for assisting with the cooking and cleaning of the facility. At the beginning, the shelter got a $5 per diem from the province for each woman who stayed there, with additional funds coming from the charity United Fund. But public and government support for shelters was growing throughout the 1980s and 1990s, with more charities contributing to their operations and even individuals giving hundreds of dollars in cash donations. In a city as big as Calgary, other shelters opened, too. CWES was sharing the workload with Sheriff King Home, run by the YWCA, and Discovery House, one of the very few long-term stay shelters in the country at the time.

But it still took work to keep the eyes of the public, and potential donors, on the issue of domestic violence. When people in the movement look back at that time, they inevitably point to the influence of one woman who created the necessary momentum to make women's shelters thrive: Carol Oliver. Oliver was a petite redhead with a passion for women's issues and an ability to bring even those reluctant to discuss domestic violence into conversations about the need for services. She was also the central figure in pushing for a new, purpose-built building for CWES, a progressive idea for the sheltering world at the time; many shelters were still operating out of donated houses or haphazardly refurbished buildings.

The new building, which opened in 1986, legitimized the services CWES was providing, says Susan Gardiner, who became the organization's executive director in 1990. This wasn't an operation that could be funded entirely through charitable donations, nor run through volunteer labour. The new building sent a message: "This was not just a project of rabid feminism. It was a societal issue," she says. Gathering the money and the support for such

---

2   Goodhand, *Runaway Wives and Rogue Feminists*, 78.
3   Peter Green, "Joyce Smith," *Calgary Herald*, January 20, 2008, B5.

a capital project was no small task, and Gardiner credits Oliver, who passed away in 2012, with making that happen.

Practically speaking, the new shelter gave residents more space to live and shelter workers more space to do their jobs. The upper level housed about a dozen residential rooms for women and their children. The main floor had counselling rooms, a dedicated office for intakes, a commercial kitchen, and a boardroom, while the basement would eventually be developed into a childcare space. Though the building would suffer major damage in a fire in 1996, for the first decade of its operation it would serve as a critical refuge for thousands of women and families and inspired passionate support from its community.

When Gardiner started at CWES, her job was to run with the possibilities the new space offered, from starting a licensed daycare for children who arrived with their mothers, to coordinating an outreach program for women who didn't want to stay at the shelter, to developing education programs for schools. There was an energy in the sector at the time, fueled, in part, by a public and governments that were finally alive to the harms caused by violence against women. In 1989, the year before Gardiner's tenure at CWES began, fourteen young women were murdered in their classroom in Montreal, slain solely because they were women working in male-dominated professions. The Montreal Massacre horrified the nation and brought gender-based violence suddenly into its consciousness.

In April 1990, Calgary Mayor Al Duerr launched a task force on community and family violence, an endeavour that landed on the front page of the *Calgary Herald* and prompted follow-up stories over the ten months it took to produce a final report. The task force had a broad mandate: to investigate violence "in families, streets and gangs, cultural and community violence, and violence against children and the elderly." Local politician Ron Ghitter, who was appointed to lead the project, stated that even without a budget to implement new programs, "this community will respond if there are problems out there."[4] That brash confidence in his community's resilience was indicative of a mood in the city at the time. Calgary had hosted the Olympics just two years prior, a wild success by the standards of the city and the world. Volunteers and paid organizers had embraced the event, taking pride in being part of an emerging metropolis that could think differently

---

4   Roman Cooney, "Fight Begins on Violence," *Calgary Herald*, April 24, 1990, 1.

and get things done—especially compared to historic centres of power like Montreal, where the 1976 Summer Games had ended over budget and mired in corruption scandals.

This tremendous municipal momentum might well have been halted when Ralph Klein became premier in 1992. After his early career as a reporter—when he had formed connections with Indigenous communities in and around the city and cast a sympathetic eye toward the poverty that many experienced—Klein defined his first years in office with budget cuts and downright antagonism toward social service spending and so-called "special interest" groups. As much as Klein portrayed himself as a "man of the people" and embraced his status as a relative of the Siksika Nation, he actively cut programs that would have helped those most in need of social support. Health care in the province was decimated under his watch, with three downtown Calgary hospitals closed. Klein led efforts both big and small, substantial and petty: his office offered welfare recipients one-way bus tickets out of province in a bid to slash the social assistance budget, while school kids worried that their extracurricular basketball or soccer programs could get cut.

But somehow women's shelters in Alberta were largely spared. Perhaps Klein was influenced by his wife Colleen's passion for the cause. Colleen Klein had survived years of violence in her first marriage and left her husband after he pointed a loaded rifle at her chest, a story she shared with the Alberta Council of Women's Shelters in the book *Standing Together: Women Speak Out About Violence and Abuse.*[5] Colleen Klein would later become a board member for Awo Taan. Or perhaps Klein was impressed by the relatively "apolitical" branding that so many women's shelters had adopted by avoiding direct links to the feminist movement. Political scientist Lois Harder has argued that creating this distance helped women's shelters "avoid [the] deficit cutting that was visited upon 'special interests'" in the 1990s.[6] For whatever reason, women's shelters were not the focus of Klein's early budget cuts. It should also be noted that the funding for women's shelters was so limited that cutting it wouldn't have made much difference to Klein's budget plans. Meanwhile, federal programs and grants in the 1990s were often sustaining the most innovative initiatives that were emerging at that time.

---

5   Colleen Klein, "I Never Look Back," in *Standing Together: Women Speak Out About Violence and Abuse*, ed. Linda Goyette (Brindle & Glass Publishing, 2005), 13.
6   Harder, *State of Struggle*, 128.

It was in this political climate that leaders in Calgary's women's shelter movement challenged themselves to develop new programs and work with new partners. Mayor Duerr's task force on community and family violence propelled the launch of the Protocol Project, an endeavour to get all family-serving agencies in Calgary to screen clients for incidents of domestic violence and develop guidelines for action if clients disclosed witnessing or experiencing abuse. Gaye Warthe, then a young social worker, was named the Protocol Project's coordinator. Warthe worked with a range of the city's agencies, including Jewish, Catholic, immigrant, public health, and youth-serving agencies. Intake workers in health settings, for example, were trained to use a version of these lines in their greetings to clients:

> We know that violence and the threat of violence in the home is a problem for many people and can directly affect their health. Abuse can take many forms: physical, emotional, sexual, financial, or neglect. We routinely ask all clients and patients about abuse or violence in their lives. Is this or has this been a problem for you, your family, or your children in any way?

Every agency would use similar wording, tailored to their work and clients. The idea was to normalize these discussions. Warthe was initially told that it would be a miracle to get even a handful of agencies to agree on a basic definition of domestic violence, let alone have them all sign on to screening protocols. But in the end, Warthe exceeded everyone's expectations and wrote protocols for sixty-four Calgary-based organizations. "It was like there wasn't anything that we couldn't do. We believed we needed to do something, and Calgary was fired up about doing something," says Warthe, who went on to become an Associate Dean in the Faculty of Health, Community and Education at Mount Royal University. "There were so many people who knew so much, but it seemed like there was still so much learning that we were doing."

That learning was happening on many fronts, from the opening of Awo Taan to a growing awareness of the needs of immigrant women. When the first women's shelter opened in 1973, Calgary was a Prairie city of about four hundred thousand people. In the decades that followed, families from India, China, the Philippines, and beyond started to settle there. The city sprawled and many newcomers could afford single-family homes with lawns that separated them from their neighbours. It may have been the suburban dream, but it was also isolating, especially for immigrant women who are particularly vulnerable to isolation imposed by abusive partners and whose cultural communities might have few ties to social service agencies. Immigrant women often fell through the cracks in other ways, too, as shelters didn't have access to trained interpreters, leaving children to take on the role of translators for their mothers.

Many women had been sponsored to come to Canada by their partners, and the threat of deportation was, as in Anita's case, frequently used to intimidate and control them. Anita was furthermore not alone in her ignorance of the existence of shelters, or what they were even there to do. To immigrant women, "[i]t seems no different than the police or state intervention they were fleeing in their country. It's just an extension of the big stick to them," Carol Oliver told a reporter in 1990, after she had been named co-chair of the Calgary Coalition on Family Violence. She acknowledged that even the most well-intentioned organizations had blind spots and preconceived notions of who they were serving and how best to do it. "We are basically White middle-class agencies that deal best with White middle-class families. We have failed to take into account the needs of immigrant women and the needs of Native women," Oliver said.[7]

But women's shelters in Calgary were learning about the needs of the diverse women who used their services, and they had the resources to address some deficits. There was community support, access to government grants, and partnerships with other social service agencies in the city—advantages that were not always present in smaller communities. Within a few years, CWES started a partnership with the Calgary Immigrant Aid Society, which offered a language bank of interpreters who could be contacted by shelter workers. Staff like Baljinder Mann, a program director at CWES at the time, worked on outreach programs to the Punjabi community in Calgary, doing presentations at the two Sikh gurdwaras (temples) in the city. She even hosted a Punjabi-language program on Shaw Cable TV called "Let's Talk About It," which highlighted topics like child abuse, elder abuse, and intimate partner violence.

---

7   Barb Livingstone, "Battered Women's Shelter Urged for Immigrants," *Calgary Herald*, April 21, 1990, J3.

Mann, who is now a medical doctor practising in Calgary, remembers hearing from people who would record the program and share it with friends and relatives who lived in other cities, from Vancouver to Regina. "I met a doctor in the shelter who had been in a very abusive situation," she remembers. "She was a doctor's daughter, and a doctor herself, but her husband wouldn't let her do anything. She heard about me from her sister in Vancouver who had seen a recording of the TV program that she had watched in a friend's house."

Perhaps the most non-traditional program that Calgary shelters decided to develop is one that still causes debate in the women's shelter movement today: treatment for men. In the 1990s, most women's shelters in the country didn't permit men to enter, either as staff members or as guests. Some shelters did not permit men to sit on their boards of directors, a requirement still in place for some shelters today. In others, older male children were not allowed to reside. Across the country, the well-being and physical health of women has always been the central mission of women's shelters, along with providing women with resources to support her next move in life.

But relationships are messy, and many women don't simply remove an abusive husband or boyfriend from their lives, full stop, once they decide to leave the relationship. Gardiner remembers that when she started working at CWES, her office was located next to the phone bank, and she could often overhear the conversations of shelter clients.

"They'd be in our offices telling our staff that they had left them and were having no contact. And at the same time, they're on the phone talking to their partners about immediate plans, or sometimes the future, sometimes fighting, sometimes trying to resolve things," says Gardiner. "They'd feel they'd need to sneak out during the day and go visit their guy. Unless we offer some real help to women where that was indicated, we're not doing them justice. They're left managing the big issue on their own. We needed more recognition that that is part of the struggle, they don't just leave in the middle of the night and never talk to the guy again. So, we felt a good way to support the woman would be to offer supports that were immediately available to their partners. And it was to get the men, believed to be in crisis, to take some responsibility for making changes."

A men's crisis intervention service started at CWES in 1991, and the YWCA Sheriff King Home started a group counselling program for men that same year. The CWES crisis service didn't operate at the shelter but at an off-site location where the spouses of women who had come to CWES could access counselling within forty-eight hours of a crisis incident. They would then be referred to other services, if needed. Iterations of these programs are still running at CWES and Sheriff King Home today. Toward the end of the decade, as Sheriff King Home planned for a major expansion of their building, the organization announced it would begin offering on-site group counselling for men and supervised visits for families in secure sections of the new facility, which would make it the first shelter in Canada to do so.

Irving Kurz, a retired RCMP officer who worked extensively on domestic violence cases and went on to manage an inter-agency domestic violence collaborative in Red Deer, recalls that at one point in the 1990s the Central Alberta Women's Emergency Shelter even funded a men's treatment program. It was a fifteen-month program called "Treatment Group for Men Who Batter."

"The philosophy in that treatment group was that you can batter with your hands, you can batter with your mouth, it's the same. The program had great results. We recognized that it was all fine and well to intervene, but what happens afterwards? How do we get women back on their feet? How do we get these guys to quit being abusive? It's not by sending them to jail, that doesn't do it in itself. It has to be through treatment, they have to unlearn this behaviour."

But proponents of the women's movement have long disagreed about what role—if any—men should have in the fight for women's rights. As Judy Rebick recounts in her 2005 book *Ten Thousand Roses: The Making of a Feminist Revolution,* women like Lee Lakeman, who worked at Vancouver Rape Relief—one of the pioneering women's rights organizations in the country—recalled that some of the most bitter disputes within the organization in the 1970s were about men. Some women were "appalled" that Rape Relief was organizing a group of men to raise money for a new women's shelter. "There were women who were convinced there was no way to work with or speak with men where men would not win," Lakeman recounts in the book.[8] Those disputes carried over into how the organization should deal with abusers. Should Rape Relief work with police, for example, to put abusers in jail? "In those days it was an either/or. Either you used the courts and fought for longer and harsher sentences, or you were against the courts. Eventually, the

---

8   Rebick, *Ten Thousand Roses*, 74.

women's movement got very good at living with the contradictions. You had to deal with both. There were men that we didn't know what to do with but lock them up, and fast. And there were men who needed to be condemned by the community but didn't need to rot in jail. We wanted women to think through the consequences and not just think like victims. The more we experience ourselves as powerful, the more we can do that."

In the Alberta women's shelter movement, those who have advocated for treatment programs for men say there's an opportunity to reach out to the other half of a relationship, especially in a moment of crisis, to get an abuser to take responsibility for his actions and be accountable to the woman he's hurt, the first steps toward making changes in his life. They argue that without helping abusers to learn different behaviours, you're not addressing the root cause of the problem. Even if women do not go back, both partners likely will find new ones, after all, and the patterns are likely to continue. But the women's shelter movement was founded on a feminist analysis of violence in the home, an analysis that seeks to centre women and avoid returning the focus, as always, to men. It argues that violence disproportionately affects women, is rooted in misogyny and patriarchal power structures, violates the bodies of women, and for too long was ignored because society considered the home a "private" sphere where the rights of women were not in need of protection. Acknowledging and working with Indigenous analyses of domestic violence—which advocates treating the family unit as a whole—has not always been easy for others in the women's shelter movement, and for some, the shift toward offering services to men is uncomfortable, too. Some shelter workers fear the feminist analysis of domestic violence is already watered down when politicians refer to "family violence" instead of "violence against women," and they say that, too often, the argument that "men are abused too" becomes cover for not providing adequate services to women.

"In domestic violence, you can't be neutral. That doesn't mean you can't be empathetic and clear, but when you're serving one population, I think you're doing an injustice to start saying we can also serve the partner," says Heather King, who worked at Odyssey House in Grande Prairie in the early 1980s.

King remembers working with a young woman who insisted she wasn't in an abusive relationship because, the woman told her, she always fought back. "I asked her, 'Who called the police when you were fighting?' And it was the first time it occurred to her that she was scared of him. She figured because she was fighting back, she wasn't afraid; that if she was fighting back, it was mutual violence. So I asked her, 'Who earns the money? How do you feel when you have to ask for money? How big is he? When you're fighting, do you think he's afraid you could hurt him?'

"I told her that fighting is not the answer and it's not okay, but battering is a different thing than fighting. It's why I still say 'battering'; it refers to a specific type of intimate partner violence and it's not lateral violence. There's a power imbalance and victims fear for their lives for good reason."

King argues that, while both parties in a relationship may need and deserve help, women's shelters need to focus on the victims of domestic violence, who require both immediate safety and longer-term support. She believes victims of domestic violence are put at greater risk of harm if counsellors and systems meant to protect women don't critically evaluate whether there is a real chance for change in the abuser. Trying to work with someone who can't change is at once a waste of resources and a danger to the partner, who might be given false hope that her partner's behaviour will improve because they're in counselling. "A portion of [abusers] think there's nothing wrong with them and are willing to get wiser and more manipulative in order to get out of facing any kind of consequences. So we're at a juncture where I think shelters need to be cautious that the victim and victim safety remain the priority."

Heather Morley started her career working at Discovery House in Calgary and later became vice president of programs and services at the YWCA. She also thinks of the women who fight back, and the way those actions can obscure the source of the violence and make the woman's danger more difficult for observers to perceive.

"I remember quite vividly early in my career, working with a woman who was charged [along with her husband] and she said to me, 'You know, Heather, I've been in this relationship for more than ten years. He hit me on probably the very first day. As time's gone by, for sure I've fought back, you bet I have. And when cops came and they arrested both of us because we're both standing there bloodied and bruised, he's still the one with the power, he's still the one who is the abuser in this relationship. So I said to the judge, Did you expect me not to fight back? Did you expect me to just stand there and take it?'" She adds: "Society is quick to jump to the idea that, 'men are abused too.' And yes, it does happen, but it's a very tricky place."

Despite the disagreements around men's programming, Calgary shelter workers were pioneering new ideas that were helping the shelter movement evolve in ways their predecessors might never have thought possible. In 1997, women's shelter leaders helped the Calgary Police Service establish a domestic conflict unit for the force, matching a similar service that existed in Edmonton. Four years later, Calgary's Action Committee Against Violence helped to launch a specialized domestic violence court, a project that pushed the criminal justice system to think critically about how it handles these cases. In the late 1990s, leaders like Karen Blase from CWES were training a spotlight on the issue of domestic violence, both in the media and in the city's leadership circles. She offered commentary, context, and analysis on high-profile platforms, which helped to galvanize the Calgary community to fight against such abuse. By 2000, eight ACWS-affiliated shelters were operating in Calgary, including several second-stage shelters where women could stay for longer periods of time.

The talent and ambition found in Calgary existed in other shelters across the province, too. With smaller budgets and fewer connections, these shelters in the 1990s and early 2000s would sometimes follow the paths being forged in places like Calgary. The Alberta Council of Women's Shelters was often a link that allowed the knowledge generated at shelters like CWES to be shared with shelters in smaller centres. ACWS held quarterly meetings, during which shelter leaders could share their learnings, leverage training opportunities, and generate new ideas. Shelters across the province were finding better ways to organize their workers, deliver programming, and—at the dawn of the Internet age—use data and technology to further the cause of helping women in need.

Carolyn Goard, left, sits at a window with a former client and her daughter in a bedroom at the YWCA Family Violence Prevention Centre in Calgary. Carolyn was dedicated to a whole-family approach to healing, and was instrumental in shifting the women's shelter movement in Alberta into the age of modernized data management.

6

"If you've got the data, they can't argue with you"

CAROLYN

Soon after Carolyn Goard started her job at YWCA Sheriff King Home in Calgary, she made a puzzling discovery. Inside a locked storage room in the basement of the building, there were dozens of boxes that each contained hundreds of yellow, green, orange, and blue forms.

Shelter staff had been filling in these forms, by hand, as Goard would learn, since the shelter first opened in 1983. It was part of the government-mandated system to track shelter occupancy and activities throughout the year. Staff at shelters across the province would fill out the forms and mail copies to the government, which would then send each shelter's annual data to the Alberta Council of Women's Shelters. By that time, in 1998, ACWS had twenty-seven member shelters and was a central voice for advocacy for women's shelters in Alberta.

"At the end of the year, ACWS would pull all the numbers together and the province would pull all the numbers together, and there was always a difference. And then we would haggle about it. Occupancy was important because government managers have to report one data point to their political masters when it comes to shelters, and that's occupancy. But it's hugely complex," says Goard.

Government officials wanted to count the number of "heads on beds" in order to determine funding, in the same way it had always done for homeless shelters. But women's shelters are all designed a bit differently from one another and operate differently as well. A woman with two children might come to a shelter and be placed in a bedroom with two double bunk beds; by the shelter's standards, the room is considered "full," even if there is an unused bed in the room.

Goard says some government officials would publicly state that women's shelters in the province were operating at 50 per cent capacity on the basis of "heads on beds," discounting the realities of how capacity limits are calculated, that placing two traumatized families in one bedroom is not good practice, and ignoring the differences between the busiest big-city shelters and some of the rural shelters with more modest caseloads.

Goard had worked as a psychologist before coming to the YWCA, where she was hired as the clinical director responsible for overseeing research development. She discovered other forms in those stacks of boxes, too, such as pre- and post-test forms from outreach work that shelter workers had been doing for years. She realized there was a lot of information contained in those colourful sheets, information that could be used to evaluate the success or shortcomings of programs. But that wasn't easy to do if the data was manually scrawled onto pieces of paper and shoved into boxes that were locked away.

Like much of the non-profit world in 1998, Sheriff King Home wasn't a particularly tech-savvy place, but it also wasn't immune to the wave of computerization that was sweeping through office environments. Around the same time, Goard had made a professional connection with a person whose work would put the shelter—and eventually other shelters in the province, too—on a path to digitization. Kelly Ernst had made a name for himself in Calgary's non-profit world with his PhD work on methods for measuring the success of social programs. He had created a database, called HOMES, for social service agencies that would enable them to do outcome measurement: social service workers would be able to assess data from their own programs and use this as a basis for making program adjustments. Ernst approached the management team at Sheriff King, asking them to consider implementing HOMES. His vision included working with other social service sectors so they could all amalgamate their data and more effectively advocate for funding and system change.

"It was an affordable program, and it was a way to get all of that stuff out of boxes. And besides, I'd been hired to do some research, and to do research, you've got to have something," says Goard. "HOMES started the road for shelters to do things like use data to demonstrate outcomes, both individually and collectively. It was a really exciting time. We started producing hard numbers that nobody could quibble with."

Other Alberta shelters followed Sheriff King's lead, and most signed onto HOMES within a few years, with the support of ACWS, which also secured funding so every shelter could purchase a computer. Shelters began to use data to tell their own stories. Instead of the government talking to the press about occupancy rates, individual shelters and ACWS could now produce annual releases about such data as their turn-away rates—the number of women who were turned away from shelters each year because of a lack of room. In Calgary alone, thousands of women were turned away from the major shelters every year in the early 2000s, and those numbers grabbed headlines.[1]

As Goard explains, "When you're delivering services to people, you collect data for two reasons: to inform your practice, and to advocate for system change and more funding. Data brings knowledge and power, because you never know what the government is going to do with that same information. Shelters and ACWS became a lot more sophisticated in using data to inform practice and tell more complex stories, with the ultimate goal being increased accountability to women and their families."

Shelters like Sheriff King began to use their own data to transform their outreach work in areas such as women's, children's, and men's group programming, and they collaborated with partners like Resolve Alberta, a Prairie-based research network focused on ending violence against women and girls. Then, a few years after arriving at Sheriff King, Goard attended a family violence conference in California that would become pivotal in informing how women's shelters operate in Alberta. One of the conference speakers was Dr. Jacquelyn Campbell, a professor at the Johns Hopkins University School of Nursing, who had studied intimate partner femicides. Campbell had also spent time volunteering at a women's shelter in Detroit, where she heard stories of abuse that included the same patterns of behaviour that she had identified in her academic studies of women murdered by their partners. "I kept thinking, 'That's really scary, but you don't seem to be as scared as I am,'" Campbell said of her conversations with women at the shelter, who described what their partners had done to them.[2]

Campbell developed a tool called the Danger Assessment to assess the risk of a woman being killed by her partner. The Danger Assessment contains questions such as: "Does he own a gun?" "Has he ever threatened or tried to commit suicide?" "Do you have a child that is not his?" "Do you believe he is capable of killing you?" Women are also asked to mark incidents of abuse on

---

1   Mark Reid, "Shelter Crisis Grows," *Calgary Herald*, March 18, 2001, B1.

2   "Jackie Campbell: Creator of the Danger Assessment," *American Journal of Nursing* 121, no. 10 (October 2021), 68.

a calendar. "You don't have to ask, 'Are you sure it hasn't gotten worse?' They can see it for themselves," Campbell says. The Danger Assessment was refined and academically tested over time, and it is now considered a validated tool to assess a woman's risk of being killed by her partner.

Goard returned from the conference determined to bring the Danger Assessment to Sheriff King. ACWS jumped in, too, to facilitate training of shelter staff across the province so they could also complete the Danger Assessment with clients. Goard says that validated tools like the Danger Assessment, combined with the action-based research that women's shelters had become known for, led to new ways of both telling the stories of shelters and keeping women safe.

Goard thinks that nowhere was this more the case than with second-stage shelters. The first second-stage shelters in Alberta opened in the 1980s in Edmonton and Calgary. Emergency women's shelters have relatively short time limits on how long a woman and her children might stay, but second-stage shelters offer up to two years of secure housing and support services. These shelters are an integral part of the support system for women leaving abusive homes, but for decades most of these operations didn't have permanent government funding contracts in Alberta. Instead, they relied on fund-raising and rent payments to sustain their operations. The first two second-stage shelters in Alberta to receive modest funding from the province—Discovery House in Calgary and WINGS in Edmonton—were considered "pilot" projects for decades.

The importance of second-stage shelters cannot be overstated; while the moment of immediate crisis might seemingly be over for a woman by the time she settles into a second-stage shelter, the threat to her safety is actually higher once she's there. At that point, it's clear the woman is moving on with a life that doesn't include her partner, and that decision can provoke an intense response from an abuser. Women who work in shelters instinctively know this pattern of danger to be true, says Goard, but the Danger Assessment helped to quantify the phenomenon.

In 2009, ACWS conducted a study of Danger Assessments in nine Alberta shelters including emergency and second-stage shelters. Overall, the study found that women at second-stage shelters had higher risk levels than those at emergency shelters; for example, women in second-stage shelters were more likely to report that their partners had used a weapon against them or threatened to do so, and they were also more likely to say they believed their partner was capable of killing them. The study recommended improved access to second-stage shelters for women and children, particularly for Indigenous women in northern Alberta.[3]

"It was a huge game-changer," says Goard, "because much of the criticism of shelters was, and I'm sure sometimes still is, that women just go to shelter to take a break. And so when you can actually demonstrate the level of risk with a credible tool like the Danger Assessment, it's hugely important."

Goard credits that research, and the dozens of reports and advocacy campaigns that came before it, for government action on women's shelters in Alberta. In 2014, NDP Opposition Leader Rachel Notley raised ACWS data on turn-aways on the floor of the Alberta Legislature, asking what the government would do for the thousands of women and children who couldn't get into shelters every year. The following year, in the lead-up to a provincial election, the party put it in their platform that they would increase shelter budgets to decrease the number of turn-aways.

"When the NDP got elected in 2015," Goard remembers, "they made good on that promise. And $5 million of new money was given to second-stage shelters. That money didn't just come out of the blue. Advocacy for second-stage funding was ongoing by ACWS since the time those two original pilots started in 1987. But when we had access to data and started producing reports in a way that we had never been able to do before, the whole couple of years before that funding came through, we were actively advocating with some colleagues in government to get funding. With all the reports that we had created, we had built up credibility over the years, and people were listening.

"We never could have done that if we didn't have the data to support our argument and the narrative. But if you've got the data, they can't argue with you."

—Carolyn Goard worked as clinical director of the YWCA Sheriff King Home for three years, before being tapped as director for the organization. During that period, she served three years as the President of the ACWS Board. After ten years with the YWCA in Calgary, Ms. Goard came to the Alberta Council of Women's Shelters as director of member programs and services. She spent ten years in the position prior retiring in 2018.

---

3   Kathleen Cairns and Irene Hoffart, *Keeping Women Alive – Assessing the Danger*, report prepared for The Alberta Council of Women's Shelters, June 2009.

✄ ✄ ✄

In 1988, Linda MacLeod—the author of *Wife Battering in Canada: The Vicious Circle*—visited Alberta to deliver a presentation for the Alberta Council of Women's Shelters. MacLeod's book, published in 1980, was one of the first on the topic of domestic violence in Canada, and it became a seminal work for understanding what abused women experience and what help was available to them. To coincide with her visit, MacLeod penned a piece for the monthly ACWS newsletter, in which she wrote:

> In times of major ideological change, history can be instantly rewritten. Shelters must be prepared to go through a period of scrutiny and possible criticism. Shelters must be ready to demonstrate positively that they do not "break up" families, and that shelters have done much to ultimately reduce wife battering by giving women the knowledge and choice to live without violence. Shelters must be prepared to shout their successes to the skies and to the press, and not to be discouraged by overt attacks or by threats of withdrawal of support. Shelter workers must also be prepared to share their expertise, to share ideas about individualized, community-based solutions.[4]

MacLeod wrote those words shortly after the Alberta government developed a standard funding model for provincially funded shelters.[5] It was a huge win for women's shelters, a guarantee they could cover basic wages and rent for their operations. But MacLeod warned that, although shelters had been recognized by government as an important social service, shelter workers would have to remain persistent in communicating the value of their work. Because with new money comes new scrutiny—not just from the public, adjusting to a new social service that acknowledges the existence and harms caused by men's violence against women, but also from government officials who would now probe the budgets and programs of women's shelters. The government

---

4   Linda MacLeod, ACWS Newsletter, vol. 2, no. 1 (January 1989).
5   The standard funding model only applied to shelters the provincial government chose to fund. Most shelters opened without a funding agreement in place; negotiations with government happened after operations had begun.

was now funding women's shelters, and officials wanted accountability. They wanted those colour-coded forms to be completed.

This shift represented the start of a long journey to enhance the services offered in women's shelters in Alberta. Over the years, this would evolve into sophisticated projects like the action-based research spearheaded by Goard, or the Danger Assessment data that was used to lobby for second-stage shelter funding. But in the mid- to late-1980s, the era of standardization started with the basics, namely a re-evaluation of the staff and spaces that had come to define women's shelters.

Women were drawn to shelter work for a variety of reasons. There were women like Lena Neufeld, who was thrown into her job at Harbour House in Lethbridge in 1986, and had an interest in social work, but no formal training. There were women like Ardis Beaudry, a homemaker who wanted to improve the lives of vulnerable women and helped to found WIN House in Edmonton, but never had to rely on her work for a steady paycheque. There were also women like Ruth Scalp Lock, who wanted to help Indigenous women get culturally appropriate help. In the 1980s, women from federal unemployment programs were sometimes sent to shelters to fill positions, whether they were suited for the work or not.

"Before it was, 'You've got two feet and a heartbeat, we'll hire you.' Now it's, 'We want to see skills. We want to see degrees or a diploma. We want to see people who are committed to the field. We want to enhance your skills by giving you training.' We want to unify the work that everyone is doing, so that across the board everyone is doing safety planning and Danger Assessments," says Kristine Cassie, who spent more than a decade as the head of YWCA Lethbridge, which oversees Harbour House.

Some women were drawn to work or volunteer in women's shelters because they, too, had experienced abuse at the hands of their intimate partners. Women like Brenda Brochu, of Grande Prairie, advocated for the opening of a women's shelter after she reflected on her own experience leaving an abusive partner and realized that some women don't have the same resources to also leave. That real-life experience was sometimes seen as an asset—in fact, in the early days of some shelters, organizers wanted a certain portion of staff to be formerly battered women.[6] That kind of stipulation fit within a radical

---

6   Larissa MacFarquhar, "The Radical Transformations of a Battered Women's Shelter," *New Yorker*, August 19, 2019.

feminist ideology, where the goal was to completely upend the social norms and rules of institutions believed to have been established by a patriarchal society that discounted women's experiences and sought to continue men's dominance of them.

But the chaos and distress of abusive relationships could seep into the increasingly professionalized environment of a women's shelter. Women facing abuse, or the direct aftermath of such an experience, could struggle to maintain the professional distance required for their work. What's more, their own extreme situations could interfere with the shelter's ability to staff itself consistently. When Marilyn Fleger arrived at the shelter in Camrose as executive director in 1986, no one talked about the fact that almost half the staff was living through abuse while at the same time working to help others escape from it. One time, police brought in a group of siblings whom she recognized as the children of a staff member. Another time, Fleger was covering the night shift when a staff member called at two o'clock in the morning to say, "My husband's just taken off drunk with my two-year-old. Can I have the next shift off?" Fleger says she encouraged the women to address their situations, but that didn't always happen. There was a lot of denial, and it was difficult to keep people as staff if they were always in crisis.

In the early years, women who went to shelters could expect to find a safe bed and compassionate staff. Workers would sit at whatever donated dining table the shelter had been able to find and listen to the stories of women in distress. But they often didn't have the training to help women assess how serious their situations were, or how to get out of them. The 1990s not only saw new demands from government, but new staff taking on leadership roles; these leaders often came to women's shelters with experience in other social service agencies that had operated for much longer within the fold of official government regulations and standards, and the accountability protocols that are required of publicly funded institutions.

This all led to moments of hard thinking about what a shelter is for: What's the mandate? How do you work to not just provide a temporary safe haven, but to break the cycle of violence? Pat Lowell was on the board for the shelter in Pincher Creek when a new executive director was hired; she remembers that the new director wanted to professionalize the service and create formal case management plans, with goals for clients and interventions for children who had witnessed violence in the home.

"We had to think about things like, 'Are we the ones to be parenting the children? Is it our job to keep them busy? Is it our job to deal with that crying child?' Because we have a mother here. If anything, maybe we should empower her to be a mother to this child in this environment. Or mom would go off and be gone for the afternoon. Maybe she's looking for a job. But what if she's coming back at eight o'clock at night and smelling like booze? We really had to think about our mandate. That we can't *just* be providing shelter. That we need to be providing intervention and assistance to help a woman, and her kids, break this cycle of violence."

When Gerry Carter arrived as executive director of the shelter in Medicine Hat in 1992, ten years after it opened, the first thing she knew she needed to change was the physical structure itself: it was an aging duplex in a rougher part of town and there was no possibility of confidentiality, since the space was so cramped. Carter remembers as many as fifteen people being squished into the one-bathroom house. She immediately looked into the organization's finances to figure out how to pay off the mortgage that came with an almost 20 per cent interest rate. She then moved on to a fundraising plan for a beautiful, purpose-built facility, which opened five years later.

But Carter was just as concerned about the high number of women who would return to the shelter for stay after stay. There were no programs or plans to get them to a better place in their lives. She wanted workers to do proper client assessments and to determine what they would need when they left, be it a contact at Legal Aid or a line on an affordable apartment. Carter says the shelter eventually worked with an assessment tool developed by the Alberta Council of Women's Shelters.

"How can you figure out what a person needs when they leave if you haven't done an assessment? It helped set goals for the client. What does she want to achieve? How can we help her get there? There were a lot of repeats because there weren't any women's programs in place. There weren't any support groups. So women would stay their twenty-eight days and they would end up coming back," she says. "We revamped all of the job descriptions and we started a training program for volunteers. There was a lot of work to do."

The number of programs offered in women's shelters grew steadily, for both clients and staff. Corrie Fortner started working at WIN House I in the late 1980s as part of a university placement program. Her job was to work with children, liaise with the department of children's services on behalf of mothers, and help those women with paperwork for the various government agencies they inevitably had to deal with. Fortner remembers working with Indigenous women, immigrant women, and White women—and she remembers that WIN House offered training sessions to help her better understand different cultures in a way that reshaped her entire way of looking at people and her interactions with them.

"It was the first place I learned about diversity," she says. "It took off my blinders in terms of what our ingrained biases might be and how that shapes how we relate to people. I learned how a banking experience could be such a different experience if you were an immigrant woman, versus an Indigenous woman, versus a woman who'd never had exposure to a bank, versus a high-level politician's wife—I learned how it could be different, and also the same. Working at WIN House was an incubator for my career and for who I became as a human being."

While women's shelters have come a long way in tailoring services to meet the needs of diverse women, the sector in the late 1980s and early 1990s was still arguably ahead of its time when it came to inclusivity and social justice issues. The basic teaching sessions Fortner attended on Indigenous culture would lay the groundwork for future endeavours, like the "Bibles, Blankets, and Beads" manual that was published in 2002 by the Alberta Council of Women's Shelters as an introduction to Indigenous history in Canada, Indigenous kinship systems, and the effects of colonialism on Indigenous people. Such efforts have continued in the years since, resulting in a range of programs, guides, and partnerships to better serve women from all communities.

When Brenda Brochu partnered with Indigenous organizations in Peace River to organize a march in remembrance of missing and murdered Indigenous women and girls, the town manager was initially lukewarm at the suggestion. "We wanted to march down Main Street. But the town manager suggested that we just go down a back alley so that it would be less disruptive," she recalls. "Lily Parenteau from Native Counselling was incensed. She told them, 'We're not going down any back alley.' We went above the town manager to the councillors and we got permission and an RCMP escort to march with us and we went right down Main Street."

Brochu's work in the sheltering movement has always been rooted in upsetting the status quo that downplays or ignores the needs of vulnerable women. In Peace River, she was learning more about how bureaucratic parameters set by the government could harm Indigenous women who came to shelters. For example, the federal government had required that shelter staff enter the Indian Registration Numbers of First Nations clients in order to receive funds, which were distributed through the province, to provide services for these women. Brochu objected to the collection of such personal information and refused to sign her contract with the province for provincial funding until the requirement to provide a status number was removed. The following year this requirement was removed for all shelters in the province.

The push to change the professional environment in women's shelters was coming, in part, from new staff with new ideas of how to run the operations, and in part from the Alberta government, which was demanding accountability. In 1989, the Ministry of Social Services developed "Core Standards" to be applied to every service under its purview, including child welfare programs, homelessness housing initiatives, and women's shelters. The department wanted full compliance by 1991. The Alberta Council of Women's Shelters became a key link between shelters and the government: it created a program standards committee to coordinate shelter-specific program standards that aligned with government principles. It later took on tasks like developing a generic funding contract for individual shelters to use with government. And research conducted by member shelters would often be used to create manuals and best practices documents to be distributed to all shelters. For example, Edmonton's WIN House conducted a research project looking into the psychological state of children in the shelter during a nine-month period in 1985. The report led to the release of a model protocol for all shelters, prepared by the Department of Family Services. Over the years, ACWS would release dozens of reports, manuals, and guidelines to member shelters, along with training programs. This continued into the 2000s and right up to today, including the training of shelter workers in how to conduct a Danger Assessment and the development of health and safety protocols in shelters during the COVID-19 pandemic.

"I took thousands of hours of training that ACWS offered because you had nobody else to learn it from. Even social workers and child welfare workers weren't taking the kind of training on family violence that shelter staff were," says Lisa Morgan, who was the child care worker at the Dr. Margaret Savage Crisis Centre in Cold Lake in the 1980s.

Even shelter directors like Karen Blase, who headed the Calgary Women's Emergency Shelter in the late 1990s, remembers the emotional support she found from other shelter leaders through ACWS. Those connections were important for those working in a sector that could take an emotional toll on staff. Blase remembers that when she first started her position, she met with two women who had previously held the same job. "They told me, 'This is the most beautiful, dangerous, and depressing job you'll ever have.' And they were right on all three counts." The work was at once fulfilling and inspiring, but also exhausting, and workers sometimes experienced secondary trauma. Blase stayed in the position for five years, and by the end, she says she was physically exhausted. "I think I stayed because I am a largely mission-driven person and the mission was so powerful and the impact was so clear."

But the changes that were happening in shelter operations weren't always welcomed by workers, or by boards. Barbara Young came to the board of Discovery House in Calgary in the 1980s and saw herself as a new type of board member, who didn't come from the social services sector but rather from the business sector. She felt board members needed to brush up on their governance models, streamline meetings, and develop more relationships with the business community. In Medicine Hat, executive director Catherine Hedlin clashed with her board on many fronts, including the issue of some board members wanting to be actively involved in the day-to-day operations of the shelter, sometimes dropping by the facility during the day. Their intentions may have been good, but Hedlin didn't think such actions were part of a board member's job description, nor did she think they were appropriate in a small community where clients might easily be recognized.

There were also instances where novice board members rose to the challenge of supporting the development of this new social service. Marta Burns started as a board member at WINGS, Edmonton's first second-stage shelter, in the 1990s. At the time, WINGS was housed in an old apartment building leased to the organization by the City of Edmonton for a nominal fee. But the building was old and small (Burns remembers attending board meetings in the basement, next to a noisy boiler that emitted loud hisses and creaks as they worked), and located on a steep hill, which made it hard for women with strollers to access. The board decided to hire a contractor to conduct a feasibility study on whether WINGS might be able to fundraise enough money for a new building. She remembers the contract was set at about $25,000. "What I remember about that board meeting is the enormity of that number for WINGS at the time. The thought of spending that much money when we didn't even know if we could raise money! I remember the whole board just sort of fearing that decision, but we decided to do it and we got the report and it all worked out fine," says Burns, who now sits as a justice on the Court of King's Bench in Edmonton. "That $25,000 expense was such a big deal for us, but later on, it didn't seem nearly as traumatic."

WINGS was eventually able to raise $4 million to construct a new building in the southeast of the city. The organization secured a $1 million donation from an estate in Edmonton, money from the City of Edmonton and the federal government, and even funds from people like Burns's grandmother, who donated $100 to the cause. WINGS expanded from twelve units to twenty. "It was something that seemed a lot like a dream, but certainly we always knew that if we just kept going forward, we'd eventually get there, and we did."

That feeling of accomplishment, and even empowerment, was occurring at both the individual and the institutional level. Just as women realized they didn't need to stay in abusive relationships, so did women's shelters, as organizations, begin to understand their strengths and power in Alberta society. According to Carolyn Goard, that progression would not have occurred if shelters had not banded together under ACWS, which lent them more clout in negotiations with government and allowed them to share resources and knowledge across the province. "The reason shelters have been so successful is because they have come together, and we have information to back up what we're doing. So, if someone in government goes off the rails and does something to imperil services for women and children, the collective can go to the media and say, 'This is not right.'"

That power of a collective and that strength of media connections has been put to the test at various times during the last fifty years. Perhaps no more so than when ACWS joined forces with a group of women's shelters that has always had an extra layer of struggle in its fight for fair funding in Alberta—on-reserve women's shelters, where the federal government and a colonial system of funding have always complicated the fight to ensure women and children get the services they need.

*Your Child Hears, Sees, Feels, Knows was a poster campaign launched
by ACWS in 2006. Aimed at Indigneous Peoples and community
members across Canada, this poster was produced in both English
and French and was intended to educate about the impact of domestic
and family violence on chidlren. This poster was produced with
funding from Indian and Northern Affairs Canada (INAC) and was
distributed to 44 on-reserve women's shelters across Canada.*

Photo reproduced with permission from The Alberta Council of Women's Shelters.

Fighting for equitable funding for First Nations shelters

CLARA

When Clara Moberly was a child, she and her siblings would run to a neighbour's house when the fighting in their home got bad. The family lived in Wabasca, one of several communities that make up the Bigstone Cree Nation in northern Alberta. The population totals just a few thousand residents and, at the time, the closest women's shelter was about three hundred kilometres away in Edmonton.

Then, one day, Moberly stopped running. She hid under the kitchen table instead. Looking back, Moberly wonders if her instinct to stay with her mother was a sign she would do something different in her life.

The first shelter on Bigstone Cree Nation opened in November 1992. Moberly remembers the Nation's social development director at the time, Gordon Auger, observing that women and children fleeing violence would often leave the community to get help. That journey was both physically and culturally difficult.

"When you're going off reserve, there's racism and you're looked at differently. If you didn't know anybody in Edmonton and you're sent over there with your four children, you're not looked at the same, you're being judged," says Moberly. "There's that mentality of, 'She's just a dirty Indian,' you know? The relationship is not there. How do you expect the person to talk to you, and to share what they're going through, if the relationship is not there?"

In the early 1990s, the Bigstone band council applied for a stream of federal funding that had opened for the creation of on-reserve shelters. The shelter in Wabasca was among the first of those to open in Alberta. Moberly had recently moved back to the reserve after studying child and youth care in Lethbridge, and she was hired as the shelter's first director. One of the first women to stay was a mother of three children. "She just had enough," Moberly says. "I think she was just waiting for something like this to go into our community, instead of her having to go out."

The shelter was housed in a four-bedroom house, with a fenced yard for children. The shelter also ran a twenty-four-hour crisis line, and Moberly had to ensure that her small staff were all trained to handle calls from anyone in crisis, including those with suicidal thoughts. Operational funding came from Indian Affairs (the federal agency now known as Indigenous Services Canada), but Moberly recalls it was just enough to cover expenses like food and basic wages. There was no money for specialized programming or support for children.

Just as distressing as the financial wrangling was the early community resistance toward the social service that Moberly and her team were running. She thinks many residents simply weren't comfortable talking about difficult issues, like sexual abuse or domestic violence. The shelter was a physical acknowledgment that those problems exist in the community and that people would be held accountable for their actions. Sensitive issues can open deep wounds and difficult conversations, Moberly says; she has some understanding for the hostility she faced.

"You were sweared at and people said things just to hurt you, like, 'Madam Moberly is running her whore house.' That type of thing. I had an incident in one of the local stores where a man came up to me and threatened me," she recalls. "I'd just say that I can understand where you're coming from. I'd just say that I empathize with him. And I tried to explain what the shelter was about. I told him, 'Look, this is what I went through. I wish somebody was there to protect me. I wish somebody would have helped me. Or would have helped my mom because this is what I saw my mom and dad go through.' That's the example I would use. There was no point in judging them, and it really helped them to understand."

Moberly still feels proud remembering how her staff persevered and how they stuck together, even through the most difficult of circumstances. "We were always very protective of each other. We had to be that way because who else was going to be there for us?" Moberly sometimes received threatening phone calls at the office. The speaker on the other end of the line would insinuate that he knew where she worked in the building. Moberly would recognize the voices. She says she'd let them talk and when she saw them in the community, she'd still shake their hands. She was willing to put the verbal harassment aside and keep reaching out to people, because she believed domestic violence needed to be acknowledged, no matter how many obstacles were put in the way of having those conversations. "These are critical issues that nobody wants to talk about. I think we really opened up a lot of doors at the time. To say, 'Hey, it's about time we start talking about this because it's not right and families need to be safe, and children need to be taken care of.'"

Moberly's mother died of a brain aneurysm two years before the shelter opened. Moberly remembers her as a kind woman who never judged anyone. She thinks that if her mother had been alive to see the shelter in operation, she would have said, "It's about time." Working at the shelter also gave Moberly the chance to reflect on her relationship with her father, with whom she maintained a close relationship, despite the events of her childhood. "I had a lot of respect for my dad," she says. "When he was not drinking, he was probably the best father. He always provided for us and protected us. He cooked for us when my mom was gone for medical reasons. But on the other hand, when he drank, he used to beat my mom up. Later I learned about the cycle of violence and I used to see it, even if I didn't know it at the time. After he hit my mom, when she had black eyes, I used to see them lie down on the bed, and he'd be holding her and protecting her. I saw all of this in my home."

Moberly planned to work at the shelter for just a few months, but she stayed for three years. One day, toward the end of her tenure, she went to her father's house for lunch. Her dad was now seventy-seven. He told her that he heard something on the radio about family violence. They had never really talked about her job at the women's shelter, but it seemed like an opening. She spoke to him in their native Cree language, and said: "I am the director of the women's shelter here, where women and children can come for a safe place. It's a haven for them because they're running away from family violence." He didn't reply.

Before she left that day, Moberly tried again. She remembers her father was sitting by the window when she asked, "Do you have any regrets? For hitting mom?"

"He didn't have to say anything. But when I sat there and I watched him. When I saw those tears . . . ." Years later, Moberly's own voice cracked as she recalled the conversation with the man who cared for her and loved her, yet who also hurt her and her mother.

Moberly went on to serve as a band councillor for the Bigstone Cree Nation. She says the community has come to accept the work done at the shelter. "It's a very different outlook now compared to that time. I'm not say- ing there's no violence, but I think the shelter is more accepted now. We've opened a new shelter in a beautiful new building. The building has been accepted. The services, the program have been accepted. I think we really opened a lot of doors. It's about time we started talking about this."

—In 2015, the Bigstone Cree Women's Emergency Shelter moved into a new facility. The shelter is now called the Neepinise Family Healing Centre. The fa- cility was named for Janet Gladue, who succeeded Clara Moberly as executive director of the shelter. Gladue served almost twenty years in the role and spear- headed efforts to open a new building to shelter women and children. Her Cree name is Neepinise, which means "summer bird" in Cree.

❊ ❊ ❊

Stand on the shores of Lake Athabasca in Fort Chipewyan and the waters ap- pear vast and endless. Turn around and the view is a panorama of thick bor- eal forest. Fort Chipewyan is renowned for its natural beauty; the stunning landscape is partly defined by its remote location in northeastern Alberta. But for women, and others, needing to leave the area, the community's remote location is a distinct drawback. For much of the year, there is no road to exit or enter by land, and the trip can only be made by plane or boat. In winter, an ice road leads 250 kilometres both north and south over frozen rivers and marshes, to the towns of Fort Smith and Fort McMurray, respectively.

Indigenous leaders for years have raised alarms that women in their com- munities must travel to major centres to get formal help to escape domestic abuse, in cities and towns that are removed from their culture and language, where it is likely Indigenous women will face racism, and where they have no support systems. But a lack of transportation options and infrastructure has meant that even women who want to leave don't always have the ability to do so. At home, the housing crunch on most reserves means that many houses are overcrowded at the best of times, which makes even informal networks of help, such as staying at a friend's or an auntie's house, an unappealing option, and makes permanently leaving an abuser much more difficult. In addition, relationship networks on reserve can make it complicated for women to seek help with friends or relatives who may have familial or friendly ties to their abuser.

In the early 1990s, five women's shelters opened on reserves in Alberta: women from the Stoney Nakoda Nations, the Bigstone Cree Nation, Sucker Creek First Nation, and the communities of Maskwacis and Fort Chipewyan finally had access to shelters in their home communities. In the early 2000s, a sixth on-reserve shelter opened on the Kainai Nation. Some of these communities are within closer and easier reach to big centres than others.

The flurry of building in the 1990s occurred at the same time that shelters in other parts of the province were starting to enjoy more social acceptance and more funding, from both government and charitable sources. On reserves, band councillors and chiefs advocated for a service they knew existed for women elsewhere in Alberta. The federal government eventually released funds to build and operate shelters on reserve, with capital funds distributed through the Canada Mortgage and Housing Corporation (CMHC).[1]

At the time, some remember, family violence still wasn't widely discussed in many First Nations communities. "When you think back, family violence was real hush-hush. Nobody talked about it. Nobody left the home when they were abused," says Joyce Badger, a founding board member of the Sucker Creek Women's Emergency Shelter, which opened in 1992. Statistics show, however, that regardless of tendencies to suppress, conceal, or accept what was occurring, Indigenous women in Canada experience domestic violence at much higher rates than their non-Indigenous counterparts.[2] The persistence of such violence against Indigenous women has meant that many normalize the presence of violence in their lives, says Janet Gladue, who served as director of the Neepinise Family Healing Centre from 1996 to 2015. One of the biggest challenges in Gladue's twenty years of shelter work was to change that way of thinking. "It's hard for some people to accept that you don't have to live like this, that there's another healthy way of living, that you can always change and have a better life."

While on-reserve shelters allow women to stay close to home and offer culturally familiar services, they present challenges relating to confidentiality that might be found in small communities everywhere, communities where everyone in town knows where the shelter is, and where there might only be one or two degrees of separation between staff and clients. "I guess there was a worry that people were going to know each other's stories. I think that still

---

1   CMHC, "The Role of Housing in Dealing with Family Violence in Canada," 2-4.
2   https://www150.statcan.gc.ca/n1/pub/85-002-x/2022001/article/00004-eng.htm

happens today," says Beryl Willier, who served as the executive director of the shelter in Sucker Creek First Nation, which is located about 350 kilometres northwest of Edmonton. "I still think people on reserve feel leery. There's the stigma they feel coming here, and that people know that they're from here. But once they get here, they're fine. With the younger generation, they're past those issues."

Shelters have become important pieces of infrastructure in First Nations communities, and they face the same budget shortfalls that affect virtually every type of infrastructure on reserves in Canada. "I can sit here and talk about our infrastructure, our capital, our housing. I can talk about everything that's on reserve and it's not the same as off reserve. That's how they've always operated," says Moberly, who went on to work as a band councillor for Bigstone Cree Nation. While other women's shelters in Alberta are funded by the provincial government, on-reserve shelters are funded at the federal level, by the various iterations of the Ministry now known as Indigenous Services Canada.

Since they first began to open in the 1990s, on-reserve shelters have almost never received funding that's proportionate to what off-reserve shelters receive in Alberta—the same disproportion that is evident in public funding for education, healthcare, and other rights guaranteed by treaty—but it took both time and collective action to clearly document the discrepancy.

Dorothy Sam, a member of the Kwanlin Dün First Nation, became executive director of the Eagle's Nest Stoney Family Shelter in southern Alberta in 2004. The shelter had a twenty-bed capacity, and Sam quickly realized that the shelter's funding was not sufficient to keep it running. "I experienced many sleepless nights thinking of how we would keep afloat," she says. "We cut back on lots of expenses and tried various things such as fundraising and asking for donations. We broke even with the fundraising and decided that it was a lot of work with not much return. We received donations from hotels for toiletries and some companies would give discounts or do work for free. We were able to keep the staff working and the much-needed shelter operating," she says. At the end of that first year, Sam recalls, the shelter "squeaked by" with a $5 surplus.

Fred Badger was a band councillor in Sucker Creek when the women's shelter first opened, and he was one of the founding members of its board. He remembers one day meeting with Solomon Yellowknee, who was on the board of the shelter in Wabasca. "We had coffee and we started talking, and we found out that we were being funded differently. So I said, 'Let's your board and my board meet,'" he remembers. "The next thing we know, the other reserves heard about it, and we decided to meet in Edmonton and we formed an organization. I don't want to say we embarrassed the feds about the funding; I don't know what word to use. We didn't feel good. We want it to be at par with the province. That was our intent."

Dorothy Sam remembers that when the group met in the early 2000s, they discussed the fact that Indigenous and Northern Affairs Canada (INAC) hadn't raised their funding in more than a decade. At that point, the group met with ACWS, which asked the on-reserve shelters to join their membership. The shelters agreed. "We brought our concerns to ACWS that we thought there was a huge disparity in funding, but we could not prove it. Jan [Reimer] asked all the other shelters if they would share their funding so that a comparison could be conducted, and that was done."

In 2005, ACWS commissioned a survey of on-reserve shelter directors in the province, which compared their funding levels to other shelters of a similar size. It found that the five on-reserve shelters were being underfunded by an average of $200,000 annually, or by more than 50 per cent; according to the report, it would have taken over $1 million to address the total funding disparities.[3] On-reserve crisis counselors earned an average annual salary of about $23,000, while women in the same job earned about $38,000 in provincially funded shelters. INAC had raised funding only a negligible amount since 1994, the report revealed. Reimer described the $1-million overall difference in funding as no more than a "rounding error" for the federal government, a negligible sum within a multi-billion-dollar budget, and yet First Nations have had to fight, lobby, and advocate repeatedly in their mostly unsuccessful attempts to achieve parity.

The report offered one sobering reality after another. "Respondents explained there is no formula to determine the amount of funding each shelter will receive, despite vast differences in capacity based upon the size of the shelters and access to resources resulting mainly from geographic isolation," reads the report.[4] "Respondents identified the secondary issue facing on-reserve shelters as the absolute lack of housing on the reserve, and that if women and children fleeing abuse want to set up a new household, they have

---

3   Tasha Novick, *Seeking Parity Between On-Reserve Shelters and Shelters Funded by the Province of Alberta*, the Alberta Council of Women's Shelters, February 2005, 8.
4   Ibid., 6-7.

to leave their families and the only community they know to come to larger urban centres." In other words, underfunding in one service area—on-reserve housing—only amplifies and complicates the underfunding in another area—crisis shelter; it's a dynamic that's repeated over and over again, anywhere that services overlap.

The data in the report confirmed what shelter leaders on First Nation reserves had always suspected. Seeing the funding discrepancies illustrated in hard numbers was an important catalyst for those demanding change, in addition to serving as the evidence they needed. "It was pretty upsetting, that they would think we're not worth getting the proper funding. We were more aware and it gave us that boost to start fighting for more funding," says Sam.

In March 2006, she and Reimer travelled to Ottawa to attend the Aboriginal Policy and Research Conference to present the ACWS analysis, and to then serve as delegates at the Federal, Provincial, and Territorial Ministers' meeting on Aboriginal Women and Violence. They were part of a national effort to draw attention to the funding disparities. The following year, the first National Aboriginal Women's Summit was held in Newfoundland and Labrador, bringing together premiers and representatives from Indigenous women's organizations. On the first day of the gathering, Beverley Jacobs, the president of the Native Women's Association of Canada, announced that the organization wanted to see a ten-year plan to reduce the number of Indigenous women who are sexually assaulted, murdered, or missing. "It's a crisis situation that we're in right now, where there's over five hundred missing and murdered Aboriginal women in the last fifteen to twenty years," she told a reporter, adding that the women were victims of "racialized and sexualized violence."[5] Jacobs articulated a direct link between the lack of shelters on reserves and the peril facing Indigenous women. "Usually, she'll end up in an urban centre living in poverty, raising her children in risky situations. She has to find a way of survival to feed her kids, so she ends up on the street, maybe missing or found murdered."

By the end of the summit, Bev Oda, the Minister of Canadian Heritage and Status of Women, announced a five-year investment of almost $56 million, with most of this devoted to enhancing operational budgets at thirty-five

---

5   Tara Brautigam, "Aboriginal Issues: Women Gather to Devise Anti-Violence Plan," *Daily Herald-Tribune*, June 21, 2007, 6.

existing shelters that serve 265 First Nations communities in Canada. About $2.5 million was reserved for the construction of five new shelters.

"It was a huge relief," says Sam. "We were happy that we were finally heard, and our pleas did not go on deaf ears. It felt like maybe we did matter after all, where we were previously ignored. It was nice to finally feel that there was some equality with funding." The money helped to provide more services in shelters and to address safety issues and allowed shelters to more consistently meet the bare minimum of service standards, from adequate staffing to the purchase of supplies like toiletries and infant formula.

For a short period, on-reserve shelters achieved funding parity with their off-reserve counterparts. But, Reimer says, that equality was short-lived; when Alison Redford served as premier between 2011 and 2014, she increased salaries for provincial non-profit workers in Alberta. Once again, on-reserve shelters were left behind.

After almost thirty years in operation, some on-reserve shelters have grown, both operationally and physically. Janet Gladue remembers that the four-room house that housed the first women's shelter on Bigstone Cree Nation was often crowded, with limited space for programming, and children were cared for in the basement while their mothers were in workshops. Gladue said it was "like a dream" to start thinking about a new space, but eventually she was able to commission plans and designs for a new, bigger building, which would include welcome improvements such as private washrooms for clients. Gladue approached the band council for some funding and then made applications through the provincial First Nations Development Fund. It took several years to amass enough grant money for the project, and the new building was completed in 2015, shortly before Gladue retired.

On-reserve shelters also developed programming specifically to meet the needs of Indigenous women and families. "Alberta's on-reserve shelters had a dream: to reclaim their traditional teachings of putting the child at the centre of their communities," reads a description of Walking the Path Together, a multi-year project by five on-reserve shelters and ACWS to offer a holistic program to interrupt cycles of family violence. Each participating shelter hired an Eagle Feather Worker who connected with families, over the course of several years, with the ultimate goal of reducing the likelihood that children would grow up to accept violence in their own relationships. The Eagle Feather Workers endeavoured to understand each family's gifts and needs, and they worked with the entire family system to address issues such as exposure to family violence, the normalization of violence, unhealthy coping strategies such as drug use, and the need for role models of healthy relationships. The Eagle Feather Workers conducted proactive outreach in the homes and communities of those who were participating, rather than waiting until clients came to the shelters for services.

More than 456 adults and children were involved in Walking the Path Together over the course of five years. The program was widely applauded by participants and organizers. ACWS had received funding through the Alberta Safe Communities Innovation Fund and National Crime Prevention Centre, but the arrangement wasn't renewed at the end of its term. "This initiative cries out for ongoing sustainable funding," states a final evaluation report prepared for ACWS. "While the on-reserve shelters are able to build on some of the tools developed . . . it is with heavy heart that we see a successful project end without a means to continue in a way that could significantly impact children exposed to violence on reserve."[6]

Meanwhile, on-reserve shelters had been adapting in other ways to new challenges that emerged over the years, such as more women facing homelessness, or struggling with mental health and addiction issues. Staff must be nimble enough to talk down someone with suicidal ideations or who is in the midst of another crisis, and stay focused on their core work to provide a safe environment for women and their children. As Fred Badger, from the Sucker Creek Women's Emergency Shelter, reflects with pride, "The shelter took in anybody, not just status Indians. Anybody who needs help and we had the room, we'd take you in. That's what I'm proud of. And that we had a good board, and the board tried to help as much as we could, to try to make a better place for clients and the staff."

Beryl Willier watched the length of clients' stays at the Sucker Creek shelter increase over time. "When I first started, women were staying maybe one to five days. Later, almost every client that came in stayed for the full twenty-one days. Some of them asked for extensions, and some of them asked to go to the second-stage shelter," she says. "To me, that means we're having a positive impact because women are getting the services they need, versus saying, 'I don't want to be here. Nobody's helping me. I feel isolated.' We're making sure

---

6   Irene Hoffart, *Walking the Path Together Evaluation - Phases I and II*, report to Safe Communities Innovation Fund, 2014; report prepared by Irene Hoffart, copyright by the Alberta Council of Women's Shelters.

we're supporting them the way they need to be supported and not trying to make them fit our ways.

"Our mandate has always been safety and change, because that's our job. We provide safety and we give you as many tools as we can to promote change. But in the end, it's still yours."

In the years since Walking the Path Together wrapped up, several on-reserve shelters have decided not to continue their membership with ACWS, stating that they want to "exercise autonomy, advocate and promote our own agenda at the federal level." But their values and teachings have informed an action plan that guides ACWS relationships with all First Nations shelters, and with Indigenous women and their families more broadly. Their teachings have also informed a high-level Statement of Principles and Values for the organization. The evolving relationship with First Nations shelters is part of a long journey for ACWS, which grew from a loose coalition of ten member shelters in 1983 to a powerhouse coalition whose scope and mandate now influence policy and public opinion as well as the lives of the women they serve.

In 2003, ACWS welcomed Dr. Jacquelyn Campbell, the pioneer who devised the Danger Assessment Tool, a powerful process of inquiry that determines the level of danger an abused woman has of being killed by her intimate partner. This groundbreaking tool helps women stay safer by identifying risk factors, reducing minimization and denial of danger, and building supportive relationships with helpers. In 2009 Dr. Campbell returned to Alberta to work with ACWS on creating a culturally appropriate risk assessment instrument for Indigenous women based on her Danger Assessment. From left to right, Jan Reimer, Janet Gladue, Helen Flamand, Alison Cunningham, Dr. Linda Baker, Mary "Cookie" Simpson, Darlene Lightning-Mattson, Sandra Ermineskin, Dorothy Sam, Delia Poucette, Dr. Jacquelyn Campbell.

A commitment for social change

JAN

Jan Reimer was out of the province when she first heard that a woman named Betty Fekete had been shot and killed by her estranged husband in the lobby of her Red Deer apartment building. The man also killed the couple's three-year-old son, and then himself.

At that time, in 2003, Reimer was just two years into her job as executive director of the Alberta Council of Women's Shelters. She had come to the position after a long career in public service, having served as an Edmonton city councillor before being voted the city's first—and, to date, only – female mayor in 1989. As a politician, Reimer had attended the grand openings of women's shelters in the city and visited other shelters throughout the course of her work. But she'd never actually worked in one, and the realities of how these facilities operate and the social systems that affect their mission were new to her; the learning curve was steep. All of those currents were present in what came to be known as the Fekete case, which Reimer first read about in a newspaper while waiting in an airport.

Blagica (Betty) Fekete separated from her husband in the fall of 2002. She went immediately to the Central Alberta Women's Emergency Shelter in Red Deer and, after her husband showed up there and verbally abused staff, she was transferred to a shelter in another town because staff feared for her safety. When she came back to Red Deer, Betty applied for sole custody of their son, the start of an almost year-long series of court hearings. Betty always applied for sole custody, but the courts continued to grant her husband some access to the toddler.

Over the course of eleven months both Betty and her husband became well known among the RCMP detachment in Red Deer. Josif Fekete filed dozens of complaints, alleging that Betty was violating a court order by not using a car seat for their son. He also complained that Betty was late for drop-offs and pick-ups. Betty, on the other hand, repeatedly told police that her husband was threatening to kill her. Two days before she was killed, she told both a police officer and a case worker from Child and Family Services exactly that—but the planned visit went ahead.

"It was such a graphic, tragic illustration of system dysfunction and the lack of respect for frontline shelter workers and court workers," says Reimer. "Betty Fekete's [husband] repeatedly threatened to kill her and at one point, he tried to run her and her friends off the road—but there's no investigation. On the other hand, he made frivolous complaints to child welfare and phoned the police because Betty's in a cab without a car seat for the little boy, and they investigate. What will always stand out for me is how a little boy was sobbing at the shelter, not wanting to go on a court-ordered visit and saying, 'Daddy is going to kill me.' The shelter workers and the court worker tried to stop the visit. But in the end, you had three dead bodies.

"I was angry—very angry," Reimer recalls. She was also saddened by the toll the case took on the shelter workers. "There was a sense of, 'If only they'd listened to us, they'd be alive.' There had been all sorts of last-ditch calls to the courthouse, to Children's Services, saying, 'Stop this visit.' And they couldn't stop it. So, there's that feeling of powerlessness. There was a lot of inertia and looking the other way by systems when it came to violence against women, with horrendous consequences."

ACWS called for a public fatality inquiry into the Fekete case, and committed to do so every time a similar case arose; Betty Fekete's death was hardly an isolated incident. The year before, a Calgary man fatally shot his two-year-old son, Cole Harder, and then himself, after a prolonged custody dispute; the child's mother had obtained a restraining order against him following an assault. A few years later, Brenda Moreside, a Métis woman from northern Alberta, called an emergency number after her drunken boyfriend broke into her home, where he lived part-time. The operator told Moreside that he couldn't be charged with breaking into his own home, and ignored Moreside's plea to send help quickly because, she told them, her boyfriend was pushing against the door she was holding shut. Moreside's body was found twelve days later.

Sometimes the province's solicitor general would agree to conduct a public hearing, and sometimes not, Reimer says. But she always wanted to put in a request and force the ministry to respond.

The deaths reverberated across the province. Minister of Children's Services Iris Evans worked with ACWS to launch a provincial roundtable on domestic violence in 2003. According to Reimer, Evans called Premier Ralph Klein and said, "You need to do something about this." A working group travelled the province, consulting with individuals and groups. The roundtable yielded more funding for children affected by domestic violence and a major recommendation from the final report was for more collaboration between government agencies, with less fighting over jurisdiction and more coordination to achieve common goals.

In the wake of the roundtable and subsequent report, Reimer decided to tackle a systems gap that she had been hearing about for years: police response. When she first started at ACWS, Reimer had heard from shelter directors who said that the RCMP often didn't take women's complaints of violence seriously; that men would accuse their wives of being mentally unstable and the situation would be flipped into a case against the woman. While there was sometimes a solid police response to complaints about domestic violence, it felt a like a "postal code lottery" for shelter workers, says Reimer. In other words, it was a matter of luck whether a police department in a particular area would take complaints about domestic violence seriously and try to collaborate with shelters. "If you had a good relationship with the RCMP, things were wonderful. If you didn't have a good relationship, it could be pretty toxic," Reimer says.

ACWS worked with Bill Sweeney, the Commanding Officer for the RCMP in Alberta, to mandate that every detachment have a Memorandum of Understanding with the local women's shelter in their area of coverage. Such protocols offer clarity for all involved: What can you do? What can't you do? How can you come together to help? Alberta was the first province in the country to develop a Memorandum of Understanding between RCMP detachments and women's shelters.

"It did make a difference. But it's only as good as the individuals that are willing to read it," Reimer says. "So much still depends upon individual relationships. Because if you have an employee who won't even come to the shelter, or they consider the shelter as the source of all their problems with vagrancy, those attitudes get in the way. Unless the system holds those individuals to account, you won't move ahead."

In 2006, as part of their presentation at an international conference on women's shelters in Mexico City, members of ACWS presented the

Memorandum of Understanding. Reimer spent several days listening to the challenges and successes of her colleagues from Central and South America. As the conference ended, there was a call-out for an organization to host the next conference. Reimer stood up and said that ACWS would do it. After returning to Edmonton, she brought the idea to the ACWS board and the group said: "Why just the Americas? Let's do a world conference."

That summer, ACWS began organizing the event, finding and inviting shelter workers from around the world to travel to Edmonton for the first World Conference of Women's Shelters, which took place in the fall of 2008. More than eight hundred women attended, hailing from Europe, Africa, Australia, South America, and Central America. Reimer clearly remembers the round dance at the opening ceremony, and a feeling that was nothing less than magical. "There was a kind of unanimity in the room, a sense of common purpose, a sense of sisterhood."

It was a representation of how women, and some men, working together can make a difference. While shelter workers sometimes change the lives of individual women, Reimer emphasizes that they also work toward systemic change. "One of the core values at ACWS, from the beginning, has been that this issue is a systemic one of women's rights. It's not only about two people's relationship with each other. There's been this vision that you're not going to change the system by yourself, that there's power in a collective. That's how we can make change; that's how we can make change for our staff and that's how we can make change for women. That's how we build safer communities."

—Jan Reimer has been executive director of the Alberta Council of Women's Shelters since 2001. ACWS works with its members to end domestic violence through culture-shifting violence prevention programs, collective data and research, and front-line training.

❄ ❄ ❄

By 2003—the year that Josif Fekete took a sawed-off shotgun and followed through on his blunt threats to kill his wife—activists and women's shelter workers had spent more than thirty years fighting for institutions and individuals to recognize the harms caused by domestic violence and highlighting the ways social systems can prevent women from achieving safety and justice. As the Fekete case demonstrated, there was still much work to do.

"Women and children are not believed. . . . Every day in Alberta women's shelters, staff see women's and children's safety minimized by the system that should support them. Abused women are often advised by authorities to keep silent about the spoken threats against them, because speaking up might jeopardize child custody. The criminal justice system listens to father's rights groups and perpetrators, putting the woman and child last in the line of authority, dismissing their truth," Reimer wrote in an editorial penned for the *Edmonton Journal*, soon after the killing of Betty Fekete.

She was writing on behalf of the Alberta Council of Women's Shelters, the organization that was first formed by a handful of shelter board members and directors back in the early 1980s. At the time, there was tremendous grass-roots energy in the women's shelter movement, but also tremendous struggle to keep these operations afloat. Phyllis Ellis, the director of the Women's Bureau, which was an Alberta government-established clearinghouse for information on women's issues, recognized the need for a provincial body to guide and serve shelters that were individually fighting to become full-fledged social service organizations. Ellis arranged a meeting in June 1981 with board members of existing shelters, and the women realized they would be stronger if they joined forces.

"At first there was no Alberta Council of Women's Shelters. That was the vision of what we wanted to become. The vision was also to get recognition from the government that shelters are a social service," recalls Loretta Bertol, the first coordinator for the organization that would eventually become ACWS.

Jean Reynolds, who led the board for Unity House in Fort McMurray, was a founding member of ACWS. She had worked with a big oil company in the northern boom town and felt she knew what the group needed to do to gain clout and government recognition: set up an office, establish bylaws, send out newsletters. The Alberta Council of Women's Shelters was formally incorporated in 1983 with ten founding members and, from the beginning, their biggest fight was over shelter funding. The organization was soon working with the province's newly created Office for the Prevention of Family Violence and, by 1986, the office stated it had worked "in consultation with the Alberta Council of Women's Shelters" to develop a "new equitable funding base for Women's Emergency Shelters."[1] However, no further details

---

1   Alberta Social Services and Community Health, Annual Report, 1985-1986, 26.

were provided. It wasn't until 1988 that the relationship was more clearly out- lined, as another government report explicitly stated that the government, in consultation with ACWS, had developed a "standard contract [that] clearly outlines the responsibilities of the Minister and the shelters, and ensures con- sistent application of the funding and program policy."[2]

"The assurance that we'd have funded staff positions was the most im- portant thing that ACWS did," recalls Marilyn Fleger, who served as exec- utive director of the shelter in Camrose in the late 1980s. "The provincial negotiations really, really made it better for all the shelters."

ACWS operated with just a handful of staff for almost thirty years; mem- ber shelters pay annual dues, but as shelters could join and leave the organiz- ation at any time, funding was variable and unpredictable. Fleger, who served as provincial coordinator for ACWS from 1990 to 1994, remembers some tense moments in those early days. Part of the problem was that, for years, every shelter was represented by one of its board members at ACWS meet- ings, with executive directors of shelters sometimes permitted to attend meet- ings but denied official board positions. By 2000, ACWS was representing almost forty shelters, making board meetings unwieldy and inefficient. In 2001, ACWS conducted an organizational review and managed to whittle its board structure down to eleven representatives, but there were still shifts in the years to come, as ACWS tried to ensure fair representation for shelters in Edmonton, Calgary, rural Alberta, and First Nations.

Despite the fluctuations, the work at ACWS was always driven by a set of strong core values: to advocate for women's shelters, to share knowledge and best practices, and to shape policy and public opinion to keep women and children safe. For smaller shelters, ACWS was also a lifeline for professional development.

"We were relatively isolated at the shelter in Peace River. We were not able to get, and still aren't able to get, many professionally trained social workers," says Brenda Brochu, whose work advocating for the opening of a women's shelter in Grande Prairie is documented in Chapter 1; she later headed the shelter in Peace River. "I'm not denigrating [the shelter employees'] work, but it was the Alberta Council of Women's Shelters that really provided that link to the outside world where we could learn about best practices and try to implement them in our shelter. We had a very good shelter here, but ACWS

---

2   Alberta Social Services and Community Health, Annual Report, 1988-1989.

was a big contributor to that. We weren't just a community shelter; we were a community shelter and ACWS."

At ACWS meetings, directors would talk about the training or programs they had managed to secure for their staff and clients, often spurring sister shelters to ask for the same. Even directors of some of the biggest shelters leaned on ACWS for support, says Karen Blase, who headed CWES in Calgary in the late 1990s. "I think ACWS was important for knowledge sharing, for emotional support for the shelter staff and directors, and for strategically linking to the legislators," she says.

In 1994, a former social worker named Arlene Chapman stepped in to lead ACWS. She remembers working with seventeen Alberta shelters when she began her tenure; by the time she left the position in 2001, just seven years later, there were thirty-five. Chapman came into the job determined to advocate for the kind of systematic changes that would improve the lives of women: "Legislation impacts the lives of every woman and child in a family violence situation. I live here. My children live here. My grandkids are going to live here. It impacts us all," she says.

One of the biggest legislative battles brewing at the time was over gun control. In the wake of the Montreal Massacre, groups led by the Coalition for Gun Control were calling for stricter regulations and more comprehensive tracking of firearms. It took several attempts by both Liberal and Conservative politicians to get legislation off the ground, such was the vociferous debate around the issue in Canada. Gun control advocates included health care, crime prevention, suicide prevention, and women's rights groups, among others. In June 1991, representatives from the National Action Committee on the Status of Women even stormed into a parliamentary committee hearing, demanding public hearings on a gun control bill being proposed by Conservative Justice Minister Kim Campbell. Some Conservative back-bench MPs were already pushing to have their own government's legislative proposal watered down, but Campbell's bill was eventually passed, and those seeking a Firearms Acquisition Certificate were then required to go through a more detailed screening process, a mandatory safety training course, and a twenty-eight-day waiting period before acquiring the certificate.

When a Liberal federal government was elected in 1993, it pushed ahead with the Firearms Act, which would require the registration of all firearms and firearm licence holders and create a new central licensing system. The Act became a flashpoint for western provinces, where rural voters hold a lot of political sway and anti-Liberal political activism is often instinctive. Premier Ralph Klein characterized the Act as an assault on law-abiding gun owners in Alberta. The issue became political and media fodder, and eventually the subject of a constitutional court challenge by the government of Alberta.

Despite this political climate, Arlene Chapman and ACWS remained staunch public defenders of gun control legislation. In 1995, Chapman presented a brief by the Alberta Council of Women's Shelters to the Senate, in which she argued, "Gun control is not about guns; it is about violence. When guns are readily accessible, they become the vehicle for expressing violence. Women are stabbed, strangled and beaten to death, but most women murdered by their husbands are shot to death. . . . Gun control is not a solution to domestic violence, but it can play an important role in preventing avoidable deaths and acknowledging that women and children, together with men, have an interest in building a society free from violence."[3]

When Alberta and other provinces challenged the Firearms Act at the Supreme Court of Canada, ACWS obtained intervenor status in the case. Chapman received hate mail, was called a Nazi, and was accused of trying to take away farmers' guns; at one point, the police escorted her to her vehicle after a conference. But she stood her ground, wrote newspaper editorials, and continued to argue that the legislation was in the best interest of women's safety. In 2000, the Supreme Court of Canada struck down the provincial challenge. But years later—and years after the registry of non-restricted firearms was dismantled by a subsequent Conservative government—Chapman is still convinced of the necessity and righteousness of her advocacy.

"Hand guns have been registered in this country [for decades]. So, if you don't have a problem registering handguns, why is there such an outcry about registering a long gun?" says Chapman. "You have no idea how many women I've personally talked to who had their husbands put a shotgun in their mouth. But let's not have gun control? You're telling me that wasn't a good piece of legislation?"

Chapman handed over the reins of ACWS to Reimer in 2001, and the former mayor was almost immediately tapped to offer comment on a number of high-profile cases involving women's safety. The public inquiry into the Fekete case attracted pages of newspaper coverage, and women's shelter workers filled the court benches during the proceedings, there to witness the

---

3   Arlene Chapman, ACWS Brief for Presentation to the Senate, September 20, 1995.

legal dissection of a case that so intimately touched the core of their work. The 2003 provincial roundtable had put another spotlight on the issue of domestic violence, and ACWS continued to maintain strong, long-term relationships with allies in the provincial government, like Iris Evans.

But sustained media attention to domestic violence is not to be expected without the ongoing efforts of its champions and allies. "Like with every flavour of the week, the week *ends*," says Reimer. "You have to continue fighting again to bring awareness to the issue."

Reimer came into the job after a period of symbolic, and financial, attacks on women's organizations across the country. Economic headlines in Canada in the 1990s were dominated by stories of the country's debt, and national funding to women's advocacy organizations across the country was slashed from $13 million in 1993 to about $8 million in 1998. There were fewer organizations advocating for women, and in Alberta most of the budget-cutting was coming from the Klein-era provincial government; the Advisory Council on Women's Issues closed in 1996, followed by the closure of the Alberta Status of Women Action Committee the following year. At the same time, the rise of Men's Rights Associations contributed to a narrative that women were actually afforded unfair privileges in Canada and that women's organizations like ACWS and shelters are simply "special interest groups." In particular, Men's Rights groups insist that men are victims of discrimination in a court system that, they allege, unjustly sides with women in custody disputes and domestic violence cases. Reimer recalls attending a roundtable meeting on domestic violence where members of a father's rights group were picketing outside the venue. They wore white hazmat suits that Reimer says were meant to symbolically protect them from women's shelters that they considered to be "a cancerous virus" or a "plague."

Threads of those narratives were amplified by some politicians in the Reform Party, a populist conservative party founded by Albertan Preston Manning, which thrived almost solely in western Canada. In 1998, Manitoba Reform MP Inky Mark called for an audit of the federal Status of Women Canada department and suggested that equal funding should be given to men's groups. "For whatever reason, men have basically been neglected. If we really believe in the principle of equality in this country, we need to be equal," Mark said in a 1998 newspaper report.[4] In the same year, an *Edmonton Journal*

---

4   Chris Cobb, "Women's Funding Unfair, Men Say," *Edmonton Journal*, October 5, 1998, A3.

editorial took aim at one of the country's foremost women's rights organizations when it argued, "Advocacy groups aren't meant to go on forever, they're meant to be around as long as their cause is pressing and as long as they have popular support. The National Action Committee on the Status of Women's best days are behind it."[5] The editorial conceded that gender inequality had been an issue in Canada, but it suggested it was time to do a wholesale review of the funding and efforts that had been working toward that goal.

Women's shelters have also faced pressures from more unlikely forces, too. In the early 2000s, several Canadian municipalities launched plans to end homelessness. These plans typically advocate for Housing First models of care, where individuals experiencing homelessness are given secure, independent housing, even if they're still dealing with addiction or mental health issues, on the assumption that a stable home is the first step toward a stable life. While the goals are laudable, Reimer says, bureaucracies start to parse housing options into "temporary" versus "permanent" housing, with the latter being the preferred investment, without regard for context or the actual length of residents' stays. Reimer thinks women's shelters started to lose their profile and opportunities for funding during that time because they didn't "count" as permanent housing, even if women actually used the services for long periods of time.

"If you have a homeless man and he stays in 'permanent housing' for one day and then leaves, that still counts [as 'permanent housing']. But if a woman stays in a safe, secure environment for six months to a year, it's not permanent enough?" says Reimer.

When Reimer first assumed leadership of ACWS, she thought she would stay for a couple of years. But more than two decades later, she continues to lead an organization that now supports forty members operating fifty shelters across the province for women, their children, and seniors who are escaping violence and abuse. Her budget was around $120,000 at the start of her tenure and has since grown to almost $2 million. In addition to supporting shelters, training staff, and spearheading research, the organization is also trying to change the cultural and societal dynamics that allow domestic violence to occur in the first place. In 2005, it launched "Breakfast with the Guys," an initiative where male leaders are invited to talk to other male members of the community about the important role men can play in the lives of women and

---

5   "Time for Review of Equity Funding," *Edmonton Journal*, July 19, 1998, A10.

girls who are living with abuse. "It was a unique way to welcome men into the conversation and debunk the myth that domestic violence is a women's issue or that it doesn't involve men," says Reimer. In 2012, ACWS launched Leading Change, which focuses on prevention through education about attitudes that perpetuate gender-based violence; the program engages schools, universities, corporations, and sports teams. It's all part of an effort to change attitudes in society, and in the process such programs have raised both the profile and the scope of practice for ACWS. The former mayor is widely credited for transforming the organization.

"When Jan came in, ACWS was a small, little provincial organization with an executive director and few other staff. That's no longer true. Jan has taken it to the next level, which wouldn't have happened with anybody but her, simply because she brought those connections from having been the mayor of Edmonton, and she was a trusted public persona," says Catherine Hedlin, the former director of the shelter in Medicine Hat. "In a lot of ways, the problems are still the same: there's not enough money; it's still seen as a women's issue; we forget about the kids; we are subject to political will, as the provincial budget changes. But I look at what ACWS is now versus then, and there's almost no comparison."

Marta Burns, a long-time board member of WINGS of Providence, a second-stage Edmonton shelter, says Reimer helped ACWS become "a voice for all of the shelters across the province." While individual shelters might have to be mindful of local community reaction to their advocacy, she says, ACWS can advocate powerfully on behalf of the entire collective.

The ACWS slogan is "we're stronger together," and the organization strives to act as a public voice on behalf of all member shelters, including those that must walk delicate lines in their political activism in order to maintain community support. It also offers a public voice for shelters that might not have the time or budget to employ communications departments or run social media campaigns.

It's all part of a four-decade journey from grassroots activism to an established shelter system. When women opened the first transition houses in Alberta in the 1970s, they couldn't have known that their efforts would create the foundation for the development of dozens of future shelters in the province. With each wave of women who pitched in to establish safe spaces for their sisters, neighbours, and friends, they learned new lessons. At first, those lessons were about basic operations: how to find a space, keep the lights on, and pay staff on shoestring budgets. The next wave of leaders took on different challenges, like how to care for children who witnessed domestic violence or how to make services culturally appropriate for the many different women who access shelter services. This work was happening as the shelter movement matured organically, as shelter workers and leaders began to see the gaps within the system they had built, but also as the government required women's shelters to meet new standards. Then, yet another wave of shelter leaders pushed for their organizations to engage in research, such as Danger Assessments in second-stage shelters, which was shared with both the academy and government to influence policy, programs, and society's understanding of domestic violence and the most effective ways to combat it. Their public advocacy also led to new programs such as a provincial benefit for those escaping domestic violence, and funding for positions such as staff to work with children who have experienced trauma.

Leaders in the shelter movement have advocated at the most prestigious and powerful government and judicial institutions in this country; they have presented their ideas to Senate committees and to the Supreme Court of Canada. But their efforts were built on a foundation that started with women who spoke at town hall gatherings, or with local politicians, or in city council chambers. Brenda Brochu attended a community meeting in Grande Prairie and declared that there needed to be a women's shelter in the booming resource town. Ruth Scalp Lock went before her city council, again and again, to get a location for a shelter for Indigenous women in Calgary. Yvonne Caouette met with the mayor of St. Paul and the community influencers at the Knights of Columbus to seek funding for a women's shelter in her small town. Carol Oliver worked connections with Calgary's business community to secure support for a new building for the Calgary Women's Emergency Shelter. It was this small-scale, hyper-local activism that established the terms and set the precedent for the high-profile, high-level advocacy that women's shelter leaders now routinely do as part of their mandate.

"For people who are involved in this type of work, it's more than just a job. It's a commitment for social change and a commitment to be a voice for women who sometimes can't speak," says Pat Garrett, the long-time executive director of WINGS. "It may not have happened as quickly as we would have liked, but I think that commitment and dedication to the movement has paid off. We all have connections to our grassroots beginnings, but we're so much more than that now. We're a vital part of the community. It's been an exciting journey."

Epilogue

LISA

Lisa Morgan was having a rough week. She was a long-time staff member at the Dr. Margaret Savage Crisis Centre in Cold Lake, whose thirty-one-year career began as a shelter volunteer. Morgan loved working with women and children, first as a child support worker, then as the centre's assistant director, and then as a coordinator for second stage housing. At times, however, the stresses of the job and the trauma she witnessed weighed on her.

On that day in the early 2000s, it all felt like too much. So, Morgan sat at her desk and penned a resignation letter.

She was mulling over what she had just written when a colleague told her someone was at the door to see her.

> I go to the door and there's this young man there—and he's, oh, six foot two, six foot three—and he goes, "Hi. Remember me?" And then, from behind him steps his mother, who I recognized. So I say, "Oh! Of course I recognize you. But you're in a way bigger body than how I remember you." So, his mom's looking at me and she's mouthing, like, "Calvin." So I say, "Is it Calvin?" He turns around and says to his mom, "I told you she'd remember me."

> Back in the 1990s, we took a group of kids on camping trips in the summer. And one of the young boys that came was a young Native boy. He biked for forty-five kilometres to get into Cold Lake to go to the camp—on a bike that had no seat! And at night he sang in his language until the kids went to sleep.

He used to be a scrawny kid, and now he was this tall man. And he says to me, "I just wanted you guys to know what a difference you made in my life, right? Going to that camp, canoeing with you guys, the campfire stories," he says. "I just needed to let you know that." And his mom says to me, "You know, Lisa, in the years since that camp, Calvin says to me all the time, 'We need to go to Cold Lake. We need to go to that shelter. We need to tell the women what a good job they're doing. And you know, say thank you and tell Lisa I appreciate her.'" Then she says, "I hope it's okay." And I say to her, "Okay, this is my story. I was sitting at my desk with my letter of resignation—it was written and it was on my desk. And then I just looked up and I said, 'Okay God, this is it. I need a sign.' Then, *ding dong*, you guys rang the doorbell. It was like a sign from somewhere that I should keep going."

Morgan went back to her desk and tore up the resignation letter.

—*Lisa Morgan retired from shelter work in 2017, but she still calls her thirty-one years at the Dr. Margaret Savage Crisis Centre her "most favourite job in the world."*

Afterword

This book came about as the result of an observation made by Jan Reimer, executive director of the Alberta Council of Women's Shelters, in 2015. She noted that the founders of Alberta's women's shelter movement had started their work in the late 1960s. More than fifty years later, these trailblazers were aging and Reimer wanted to ensure their stories were preserved.

In the years that followed, ACWS organized interviews with dozens of women, and some men, who played a role in shaping the province's shelter movement. ACWS extended invitations to former and current shelter workers and board members from across the province.

Those interviews form the basis for this book. Women involved in the shelter movement offered anecdotes and general recollections about their work, along with analysis of the social and political context in which it was carried out. Their stories are an important part of Alberta's history and contribute to our broader understanding of the feminist movement in this province.

The stories presented in this book represent only a small sample of the many women who played a role in advancing the women's shelter movement in Alberta. Regrettably, not every person who participated in the interview process could be quoted in the text. But whether quoted or not, every interview helped to shape the overall narrative.

In addition, there were several shelter leaders who passed away before they could be interviewed. In some of these cases, their colleagues paid homage to them in the stories they chose to share. Still, it is inevitable that the good work of some women has not been represented fully here.

Women's shelters in Alberta have been shaped by the work, dedication, and convictions of hundreds of women over the past five decades, be they staff, volunteers, or board members. It would be impossible to capture all of their individual accomplishments, but this book is an attempt to highlight how the sum total of that work became a powerful feminist social movement.

A woman sweeps in the kitchen of an early shelter house.

Author Acknowledgments

This book would not have been possible without the knowledge, guidance, and vision of the senior leadership team at the Alberta Council of Women's Shelters. This project was conceived and driven by their conviction that Alberta women's stories deserve to be recorded and celebrated—I couldn't agree more.

I am equally grateful for every person who agreed to be interviewed for this project. I appreciate how candidly they shared their stories, and I wish I could have quoted every participant in the text. I am so very lucky to have been entrusted with their personal stories, which helped me to understand how individual actions and convictions can build a society-changing movement.

I would also like to thank my editor, Rachel Hertz-Cobb. Her critiques and edits of my manuscript made this book infinitely better. I feel lucky to have worked with such a talented editor, who put such immense care into working with my writing. I am also grateful to Brian Scrivener and the University of Calgary Press for their support in publishing this book.

And finally, I want to thank my family—Tej and Arjun. They listened to me think out loud about the flow of my text and offered suggestions on the wording of many sentences. But most important, they believed that I could write this and told me they were proud. I'm not sure I could have finished this book without them.

Sources

Annual Report. Edmonton: Alberta Social Services and Community Health, 1985-1986.

Annual Report. Edmonton: Alberta Family and Social Services, 1988-1989.

A Proposal for Change to Aboriginal Family Violence. Thunder Bay: Ontario Native Women's Association, 1989.

Bielski, Zosia. "A Simple Hashtag Reveals the Complexities Facing Women Who Experience Domestic Violence." *Globe & Mail*, September 9, 2014.

Brautigam, Tara. "Aboriginal Issues: Women Gather to Devise Anti-Violence Plan." *Daily Herald-Tribune*, June 21, 2007.

Boyce, Jillian, *Victimization of Aboriginal People in Canada, 2014.* Ser. 85-002-X201600114631. Ottawa: Statistics Canada, 2014.

Cairns, Kathleen, and Irene Hoffart. "Keeping Women Alive – Assessing the Danger." Edmonton: The Alberta Council of Women's Shelters, June 2009.

Calgary Herald. "Gerri Many Fingers Community Service." June 19, 1994.

Calgary Herald. "Women could set own political rules." June 18, 1973.

Calgary Herald. "Women's Lib helps Black Men Too—MLA Rosemary Brown." April 12, 1973.

Canada, Canadian Centre for Justice Statistics, *Family Violence in Canada: A Statistical Profile.* 2016.

Canada, House of Commons, Standing Committee on Health, Welfare and Social Affairs, *Wife Battering: Report on Violence in the Family.* May 1980. https://parl.canadiana.ca/view/oop.com_HOC_3201_19_5/1.

Canada, Privy Council Office, *Report on the Royal Commission on the Status of Women.* 1970. https://publications.gc.ca/site/eng/9.699583/publication.html.

Canada, Canada Mortgage and Housing Corporation, *The Role of Housing in Dealing with Family Violence in Canada.* 2012.

Chapman, Arlene. "ACWS Brief for Presentation to the Senate." September 20, 1995.

Cobb, Chris. "Women's Funding Unfair, Men Say." *Edmonton Journal*, October 5, 1998.

Collins, Erin. "Alberta's Dirty Little Progressive Secret." *CBC*, December 17, 2015.

Cooney, Roman. "Fight begins on violence." *Calgary Herald*, April 24, 1990.

de Lesseps, Suzanne. "Women Push for Rights." *Calgary Herald*, June 21, 1975.

Edmonton Journal. "Shelter for battered women opens." December 6, 1978.

Edmonton Journal. "Time for Review of Equity Funding," July 19, 1998.

Fateaux, Nicole. "Jackie Campbell: Creator of the Danger Assessment," American Journal of Nursing 121, no. 10 (October 2021).

Ferguson, Eva. "Out from the shadows." *Calgary Herald*, March 11, 1993.

Garrett, Rick. "Order of Canada Recipients Well-Deserving." *Anishinabek News*, January 5, 2018.

Green, Peter. "Joyce Smith." *Calgary Herald*, January 20, 2008.

Gold, Marta. "Time for a Change, WIN House Director Says." *Edmonton Journal*, July 2, 1988.

Goodhand, Margo. *Runaway Wives and Rogue Feminists: The Origins of the Women's Shelter Movement in Canada*. Winnipeg: Fernwood Publishing, 2017.

Goyette, Linda. "Gov't Pays Women Less, Report Says." *Edmonton Journal*, October 15, 1979.

Harder, Lois. *State of Struggle: Feminism and Politics in Alberta*. Edmonton: University of Alberta Press, 2003.

Heidinger, Loanna. *Intimate Partner Violence: Experiences of First Nation, Métis and Inuit Women in Canada*. Canadian Centre for Justice and Community Statistics, 2018. https://www150.statcan.gc.ca/n1/en/pub/85-002-x/2021001/article/00007-eng.pdf?st=rnnvytbZ.

Hoffart, Irene. *Walking the Path Together Evaluation – Phases I and II. Report to Safe Communities Innovation Fund 2014*. Edmonton: The Alberta Council of Women's Shelters, 2014.

Janovicek, Nancy. *No Place to Go: Local Histories of the Battered Women's Shelter Movement*. Vancouver: UBC Press, 2007.

Klein, Colleen. "I Never Look Back." In *Standing Together: Women Speak Out About Violence and Abuse*, edited by Linda Goyette. Edmonton: Brindle & Glass Publishing, 2005.

Koenig, Wendy. "Price of Peace at Home May Be Too Costly." *Edmonton Journal*, January 4, 1979.

Livingstone, Barb. "Battered women's shelter urged for immigrants." *Calgary Herald*, April 21, 1990.

Locherty, Lorraine. "Violence 'Joke' Sparks Furore." *Calgary Herald*, December 17, 1988.

MacFarquhar, Larissa. "The Radical Transformations of a Battered Women's Shelter." *New Yorker*, August 2019.

MacLeod, Linda, and Andrée Cadieux. *Wife Battering in Canada: The Vicious Circle*. Canadian Advisory Council on the Status of Women. Hull: Canadian Government Publishing Centre, 1980

Maracle, Lee. *I am Woman: A Native Perspective on Sociology and Feminism*. Richmond: Press Gang Publishers, 1996.

Menzies, Heather. "Liberation in Low Gear." *Edmonton Journal*, December 30, 1975.

Mildon, Marsha. *WINning: The Trials, Tribulations, and Triumphs of Opening a Women's Shelter*. Edmonton: Housing for Women Book Society, 2020.

National Inquiry Into Missing and Murdered Indigenous Women and Girls. *Executive Summary of the Final Report*. Vancouver, 2018.

Nickel, Sarah A. "I Am Not a Women's Libber, Although Sometimes I Sound Like One." *The American Indian Quarterly*, Vol. 41, No. 4 (Fall 2017): 299-335. University of Nebraska Press, 2017.

Novick, Tasha. *Seeking Parity Between On-Reserve Shelters and Shelters Funded by the Province of Alberta*. Edmonton: The Alberta Council of Women's Shelters, February 2005.

Ottawa Citizen. "Male MP's Guffaws at wife beating query enrage female MPs." 1982.

"Proposal for Women's Interim Aid," Nagisayway peygamak (no date). Document courtesy of WIN House Archives.

Rebick, Judy, *Ten Thousand Roses: The Making of a Feminist Revolution*. Toronto: Penguin Press, 2005.

Reid, Mark. "Shelter Crisis Grows." *Calgary Herald*, March 18, 2001.

Scalp Lock, Ruth and Jim Pritchard. *My Name is Shield Woman: A hard road to healing, vision, and leadership.* Charleston: Day Time Moon, 2014.

Speirs, Rosemary. "Lacklustre hearings dull and repetitive." *Calgary Herald*, September 19, 1968.

Supreme Court of Canada, Murdoch v. Murdoch, [1975] 1 S.C.R. 423, 1973.

Sweetman, Keri. "Male MPs' Guffaws at Wife Beating Query Enrage Female MPs." *Ottawa Citizen*, May 13, 1982.

Trimble, Linda. "The Politics of Gender." In *Government and Politics in Alberta*, edited by Allan Tupper and Roger Gibbins. Edmonton: University of Alberta Press, 1992.

YWCA Alberta Action Committee, *The Mossman Report on Housing Needs in the City of Edmonton for Homeless Girls 15-25 Years of Age.* Edmonton, 1969.

About The Alberta Council of Women's Shelters

Together, The Alberta Council of Women's Shelters (ACWS) and its members work to end domestic violence—in our homes and throughout our communities.

A registered charity, ACWS is the provincial network organization of domestic violence shelters in Alberta. We bring close to four decades of experience and knowledge to serve our 39 members operating over 50 shelters across the province for women, their children, and seniors facing domestic abuse. We advocate for ACWS members and work with them to end domestic violence through culture-shifting violence prevention programs, collective data and research, and front-line training. With support from ACWS, Alberta shelters are helping to provide safety, support families, and improve communities.

Domestic violence remains a serious and urgent problem in Alberta. Collectively, we are challenging the harmful beliefs and actions that perpetuate domestic violence in our communities.

For more information, visit acws.ca.

Founders of the Edmonton Women's Shelter gathered at All Saints' Cathedral in 1995, 25 years after it opened and housed the first shelter beds in the city. Sitting, from left, Jessica Hanna, Lynn Hannley, Phyllis Ellis, and Ardis Beaudry. Standing, from left, Daisey Wilson, Lucille Ross, and Betty Nigro.